Diary of a Wimpy Eventer

Part Two

How to stay on top

If you've made it to this second book
there will be things that have now stuck.

This book will only reaffirm
that 'chip p*ssers' is a valid term.

You **must** still keep an open mind
and stuff your posh and too refined.

For in this book there will be swears
and curses, tears and greying hairs!

www.wimpyeventer.com

The moral right of the author has been asserted.
Printed in Great Britain.

Written, designed and produced by Gary and Victoria Brant
(Daddy Carrot and the Wimpy Eventer)

Beautifully illustrated by Bonny Snowdon Fine Art

Edition 1
ISBN: 978-1-5272-1760-7

With thanks to…

I feel so different writing this than when I wrote the first one. I owe that feeling to my husband. Gary, my Daddy Carrot is without question, the most supportive, understanding and devoted husband and best friend I could ever wish for. Endless nights he has endured my 'eyes on mobile phone' attention deficit, watching me write blog posts and then proofing them, following me around the country in pursuit of my missing balls of bravery. I owe him this paragraph at least!!

But once again, I would be nothing without all of you. Every single one of you reading this has taken a chance, a chance to believe in something that I know exists. You are the reason I still do this, I hope once again that I make you proud.

INTRODUCTION

You cannot change what has already been, but you can make what hasn't happed yet downright bloody brilliant. You have that power, the power to change YOUR tomorrow – what is it that you're waiting for?

My adult life has taken so many turns that I hadn't seen coming, so many things I haven't stuck at, jobs I have complained about, people I have lost touch with. But let's get one thing straight, to move forward you must have dealt with things in your past and put those things to one side in order to be content in moving on.

♥ Posts marked with this heart are ones poured in from the Diary of a Wimpy Eventer Facebook page.

IN THE BEGINNING

I don't really remember a time when I haven't had a mind filled with horses. Some of my earliest memories are of Skegness beach donkeys and a hand me down Sindy horse from my cousin that was a firm favourite in my pile of things. I never had ponies or parents that were remotely interested in the sport of equestrianism. But, whilst I had these loose connections with plastic horses from a young age (and hours spent riding Dobbin, my homemade wooden pony), I hadn't actually been lucky enough to clamber onto one until I was six years old.

I expect part of my continued love of horses beyond the first throes of passion stemmed from mild jealousy. At six years old, my closest friend began pony riding at the local riding school, she smelt of wet wax jackets and I didn't; but I wanted to. I wanted to get red faced and come home with a welly full of wood shavings. I begged my poor parents for the opportunity, over the course of a few days, probably knowing that £6.50 a week for a hobby (likely a short lived one) was a bit much for them 25 years ago. But alas, it worked, I was allowed to go! And go I did, I embraced it all. I wasn't one of the kids that came for their ride and b*ggered off after an hour, not me! I got royally stuck into mucking out, poo-picking fields, filling water buckets and it was then that we agreed with the yard owner that I would get a discounted rate for helping all day. I would spend all Friday evening planning the rides for all the other children that were coming along and writing "I love INSERT FAVOURITE HORSE'S NAME" in the margin.

Saturday at 8am was the best time of the week. I would pull on my new beige jodhpurs that were 3 sizes too big and handed down from the family my mother cleaned for. I didn't care, I had my own 'jogpers'. I found a riding hat at the car boot sale a few weeks later, this was when my parents realised my new hobby wasn't going to be as short lived as they would have liked. Lord knows you are probably all cringing right now – allowing your small child to get on a horse in a helmet that barely had a harness and that smelt like a nest box for ferrets. This was the early 90's, standards for helmets were looser then and the rubber chin cup protector made me sore so we cut it off!! Oh and the wax jacket, I had one given to me, it was too big and the sleeve inners were hanging out the ends of the arms but I smelt of *that* smell… and I loved it.

One of my very first memories of riding was probably one that set me up with courage for a good few years, but equally one that could have broken me in two…

Pulling on my 'jogpurs' and gabbing my ferret smelling riding hat, I went to the stables as normal on my long awaited Saturday. The lady waited until all the Mums and Dads had left and dragged out this little bay pony from the field, he looked nice enough – I remember he had a friendly face.

Saddled up, I was asked to get on and I was very firmly told that if I fell off, I wasn't allowed to ride her ponies ever again. I must have been shocked because I agreed to this deal and held on tighter than ever… Good job I did because she walloped the pony up the backside with a plastic shovel and sent it flying up the field! He knew the drill and stopped at the end, I walked him back to the lady and she seemed fairly impressed! I felt very good that day! I felt proud in front of all the other children that were cowering awaiting their turn. I look back now and it became very apparent that that day could have changed EVERYTHING. I could have been a dancer or a gymnast or a chess player… but no, I held on tight and it filled me with the biggest sense of pride I had ever felt. The danger, the speed, the desperation to not let people down… all the things that still keep me going and pump adrenalin through my veins on a show day.

Funny how things seem when you look back, I always think of those days at the stables and how wet through I was! I fell in love with horses though and I didn't care about the wet or the cold. After three years of weekly pony rides, summer camps and learning the ropes on the yard, I found my one true love… He was perhaps an unusual first love for a little girl, he was stocky and opinionated and was my biggest challenge to date, but that was the best part.

A few years passed, and I had ridden all of the ponies in the riding school and had dedicated so much time to bareback riding, galloping and jumping that when the owner came home with a £200 gypsy cob she had bartered for with the travellers in the village, I knew we were going to be a team. Django was rising 4, barely broken to ride and my first experience of getting on him was trying to get him home. I got legged up on to a Polypad strapped on with an elasticated band (we didn't have a saddle for him yet) and the owner from the car behind us swung a lunge line at him to get him going! And go he did, vertically! He reared, that's why they had sold him. I wasn't frightened though, not one bit. I loved the feeling of wrapping my skinny arms around his neck when he stood up, I growled at him and feebly smacked his bottom and with a bit of time he just got better and better. We went hacking often over the summer holidays and then the day came… I remember it so very vividly, the first time I was truly scared on a horse.

It was pivotal. I'd never felt fear, nerves or palm sweating before. We had been jumping Django for a little while now and my goodness he could fly, 1m25 at the 'Chase me Charlie' competition was nothing for him and at only 13.2hh I felt this was a good achievement. Now, one particular day we hacked across the stubble and it was casually suggested that I jump him over a straw bale that was waiting to be collected from the field. It was easily 4ft high, the same wide and it was right there that I felt it. I mentally dared myself to jump it and as I circled my legs just froze, I had bailed out in my mind and he refused. What was happening? I came again, and the same thing happened. I couldn't kick, I felt paralysed. The owner made me get off and put an older, braver girl on my beloved Django and he just soared it. I felt destroyed, I cried all the way home in the car and I don't think I went back for a few weeks after that. I couldn't work out why my body failed me, I wanted to give up. So young, I think maybe 11 years old, I felt fear and failure in a horrible bundle right there. I did go back though, and I did carry on as though everything was ok but I knew it wasn't, not 100%. There was always a niggle and I felt different, just at the right moment the lady put the price up to £10 a day and my parents decided this was a bit too much money. I was secretly a little bit relieved.

It wasn't long before I missed my wax/ferret scent and I began helping with the hunt horses at the local stables. With the experience and hard working attitude I had, I was allowed to sweep the whole yard in return for a ride up the long drive and back most days. These horses were MUCH bigger than what I was used to, the smallest being 15.3hh and the biggest at 17.2hh a long way up after nothing bigger than a pony! I progressed quickly though and learnt to ride the smaller of the bunch, hacking out regularly and helping as often as I could with tack cleaning and more sweeping. That hard work paid off and I remember it so vividly, the day when I was asked if I would like to go hunting. Very soon, I fell in love again. I was loaned all of the clothes I had to wear for the hunt. I was very lucky because there were lots of pairs of jodhpurs and hunting coats, now outgrown and waiting to be de-mothballed and enjoyed in the big cupboard in the tack room.

I loved hunting, I loved the early mornings of getting them ready, radio on cleaning them up and mucking out the stables just in time to devour the leftover cooked breakfast that was waiting on top of the Aga in the big house. I'll never ever forget how amazing the scrambled eggs were for as long as I live! Getting to the hunt meets I never felt nerves, just cold! I remember being freezing and foot followers wrapping their spare coats around me when we were standing for a while. Hunting people are some of the nicest I have ever come across, they really look after each other and I loved that feeling of being part of something.

I look back now and remember crisp bright days and autumn hunting, not rain or dark days like before. I used to get changed in the toilets after school for the horsebox to pick me up from the gates to go evening cubbing. Oh! I felt so lucky. My mother was (and still is) the house keeper in the big house which boasted this traditional hunting stables. It's walls; black bitumen bottom halves and white wash top halves, a Burco boiler filled with sweet smelling boiled barley and 12 fully clipped, shiny steeds- I did secretly long for a hairy pony or gypsy cob but they were wonderful nevertheless.

The groom in this yard was so much fun, she taught me so much and I will remain grateful to her for as long as I live. Emma was and is still the most knowledgeable horsewoman I have ever met. Traditional horsemanship was paramount, knowing how to care for these athletes, the canvas New-Zealand rugs, feeding straits like plain oats and rolled barley, breaking horses WELL (not just shooing them with a lunge line!) and foaling at least one every year, the list of things I learnt was extensive.

We had fun on the job and one summer we had a particularly sharp 4 year old to back which was proving a little bit tricky. Improvisation tactics took us on a trip to Ann Summers to buy ourselves a jockey that wasn't scared to get on….! We arrived back that afternoon and after inflation, dressed our jockey's ample naked body in some overalls, body protector and gloves and named him Oliver Overall. He wasn't the best at staying upright but we bound him to the saddle and added some weight in sand bags and it was only when his erratic bouncing head smacked off the corner of a wall that he slowly deflated and needed a patching up!

I spent nearly 5 years sucking up this limitless knowledge like a sponge. I covered days off and had my first real paid job. Having the yard to myself and managing just for one day – I'd have done it for free, Sundays were just brilliant, that was my day.

Hunting days were brilliant too, whilst the family's children were at boarding school I got to ride on a beautiful palomino mare called Flossie, Highfield Gold Candy Floss. I was in love again. We even attended Pony Club rallies and camp one year too! I sometimes lied to the other children and said I lived in that big house and owned all those big shiny horses, I felt great and I look back now and still do feel great. It was magical. Flossie wasn't very confident jumping and quite often I would come over her head in front of the jump and have to run back to the box for a new pair of reins, but she taught me to stick on like glue. I remember being out hunting, just standing at a covert and her entire bridle being pulled clean off by another horse and no one noticing until we moved off!!

I laughed often in this yard and my dear teacher made this magical for me, she restored my faith in my own ability and gave me knowledge which inevitably breeds confidence. I still speak to her often for advice, guidance and reassurance, but the difference is, I can offer it back now too, because we are the same. Oh! The stories I could tell… but that's not why we're here, I was 17 and equipped with knowledge, I rode at an above average standard and I knew fear, but I was definitely not afraid.

Knowing and dealing with fear is all you can do when you see the other side of 30 and decide to go eventing, things are VERY different now!

A LIFE LESS ORDINARY…

With the first event under my belt, and at 90cms not the rained off 80cms I had planned, I felt decidedly happy driving back to get my sheet only to find that we had been placed 7th! I can't even begin to describe what it means to get one of those top ten coveted spots that people work so hard for. It's hard to believe that we were good enough (or jammy enough) this early on to be awarded this slot in the rankings, especially as we had two poles down in the show jumping. Fluke perhaps… The hard work that goes in to even just getting to that first event, I HAD practiced hard since the 1st of January and I HAD got Pat plenty fit enough for our quest, I think that's why I burst into tears at the very thought of getting a rosette – sheer exhaustion!

♥ Friday, April 7th 2017 – *we have only 3 weeks until CHILHAM BE and I'm on the Waitlist so I won't start pooing my pants just yet! Or will I?!*

The next few events were looming and one of the most awful things is having to enter weeks in advance. The only thing I can liken the feeling to is having my wisdom teeth removed (or not!) I got the date weeks in advance and bailed out twice before committing to a lifetime of paracetamol to avoid the dreaded fate of the dentist! – I still haven't had them out!!

Oh! How I longed to go back to that feeling I had at 17, eventing and hunting to my heart's content. I felt no real sense of fear, just competitive spirit and the grit and determination you need to love the sport. I was so balls deep in horses back then, but everyone was talking about University and I thought it best to have a think about my future, my career and what I planned on doing when I was a grown up! I'll tell you what, I'm 31 now and I still have no idea what I want to be when I grow up, if I grow up!

I decided I would take a course in Equine Sports Science a BSc, which after 6 weeks of being taught how to pick feet out and the most basic of biomechanics and nutrition, I soon learnt that this was definitely not for me and BSc stood for 'Big Sack of Crap'. There were some students on the course who had never even led a horse, this was not for me and my limited patience. I had skills and experience and as an over-confident nearly 18 year old, I thought I could teach the class a thing or too myself!

That's it then… too late to get enrolled on another course, too stiff to join the circus; I was on a GAP YEAR! I wasn't spending my money going travelling though, it would have probably only got me to Skegness pier, having never been a saver. I was skint, unemployed and in love with horses!

Lucky for me the groom at the hunt stables got married and moved away and as with fate, I took the job full time for a year. It was perfect timing and utterly magical. I loved running the yard, writing fitness plans, drawing up feeding charts and spending every waking hour smelling of horse sweat and urine. I was in heaven. I did know that it wasn't a forever job though, as other horsey people I had often told me; "You need to marry rich or have a back-up plan…" ! I didn't have much time for men so back up plan it was!

The following year I went through UCAS clearing (a system designed to aid the disorganised or disappointed!) and with my decent enough A level results, I took a space on a course called Marketing and Public Relations; a BA. I had no idea what marketing was and had absolutely no desire to relate to any kind of public, but it sounded better than bio-engineering! I started the course and by week three I felt despondent, I lived at home and didn't feel I fitted in with the others (story of my life!). I wasn't the student type – I didn't like drinking cheap spirits from a mug or eating packet noodles for days on end. I like my Mum's Yorkshire puddings and I was a rural recluse deep down, I enjoyed my own company from such a young age that my late teens were no different. I remember sitting in my Biology A Level exam with my arms covered in blood and placenta from foaling in the early hours… I got off to a bad start on the fitting in stakes, I think maybe it was scent related?! I did have a large group of friends at big school though and always played the clown card, I wasn't pretty enough to be popular for that, I wasn't clever, not really. I was just different to everyone else and I regularly used that to my advantage.

In my first couple of university terms I wasn't attending much, I had taken a little job on a private yard which is obviously where I would rather have been, but consequently I wasn't learning much either and when assignment and exam dates loomed I ended up teaching myself using online tutorials! It wasn't all bad, my own learning techniques had me coming out with some of the best marks in the class! I figured I'd scrap seminars and go riding instead, I was still doing ok.

By February of the first year I could smell the holidays looming, I would break-up at the end of April and didn't have to be back until September other than for paper tests, the world was my oyster. I just so happened to be sat on the train that day, open on the careers section of the Horse & Hound magazine which back in 2002 was at least 2 pages worth of screaming opportunity…!! A different path to tread, one that takes me out of my comfort zone and anyway, don't they say 'change is as good as a rest'?

MENTAL PREPARATION

Change is only ever as good as a rest if your change isn't going from spending 2 years only doing flat work in a confined area to then attempting to gallop and jump in an open field!

♥ **<u>Monday, April 10, 2017</u>** - *Selling yourself in less than 100 words can only be done if you truly believe in these five - I can and I will.*

Mentally preparing yourself for things that require your full concentration and for things that mean something to you, takes determination. At times I have lacked lustre and felt ever so slightly not good enough. I felt it a little bit when I look back at my first event of the season at Munstead. I remember feeling so confident in the show jumping warm up, chatting to my friend Alfie and then getting in the ring and freezing like a Mini Milk in Antarctica… I was paralysed again.

This fear paralysis makes me ride like a total turd and there is so little I can do to snap out of it at the time. It's almost like I'm not aware it's happening until I look back. I think the only way to get through this feeling of bum twitching paralysis, is to do it more. Make the muscle memory that of confident and capable riding not foetal uselessness, that was what I set out to do after Munstead. I booked 2 lessons, went unaffiliated show jumping TWICE and didn't fluff it up too much. Stage fright is awful, but stage fright on a spooky horse, knowing you could get injured is far worse. I am dealing with it, but it's not an overnight fix.

Was I really ready for a late entry into another event? It popped up on Facebook that there were spaces left in the BE90 and so with only a week to go, I entered last minute into the BE90 at Bovington. Borderline too far for me to travel with my inexperienced livestock movements (horsebox driving) but b*gger it!! We were entered, after all that practicing I felt like I wanted to see if I had got any better.

At this point I will just point out that I DO NOT have pots of cash hidden away for entering shows and each event for me means; entry fee (around £80), lorry hire (£100,) fuel (£40), start fee (£15) and money to keep Daddy Carrot in chips and buy a photo at the end (£20)… that's over £250 PER EVENT! For this one I had a ruddy good clear out of my excess stuff and had a mass eBaying session to pay for it! I also had a bit of birthday money left, so we weren't eating beans too often!

Don't ever think for a second that you get anywhere in life without sacrifice and hard work. I have worked so hard for my season this year and not just getting the horse prepared, simply affording it has left me battling palpitations and exhaustion, would I have done it differently? Unlikely! I have a point to prove, a challenge to face and a battle with fear to conquer – it makes money seem meaningless and I'd have done anything to keep going!

EVENT REPORT – Bovington BE90

So here it is, Number 2! The late entry into the BE90 at Bovington, Dorset (RAC Saddle Club Bovington) on Easter bank holiday weekend was our challenge. Now for anyone that knows me, I'm not overly keen on jumping around somewhere that I'm not overly familiar with, stupid eh?! But I like to have had a school round to feel confident enough to know the ground and at least a few of the jumps.

Bovington for us, is about 2.5hours away, I was crapping it!!! Not just about the long journey but the unknown territory and the impending death. I'll quickly roll back to Wednesday, where we had a super session with my new hero, Russell Cooper. Long story short, I cracked the Pat Pony code that I've been trying to crack for 5 years!! Albeit nearly getting launched out the saddle in the interim!!

Now I thought as a reward, he could have a couple of quiet days and when I came to hack on Saturday, he was awful!! I mean awful awful!! Spooking at EVERYTHING!!! Argh!! You can't get mad or upset, it just makes it worse. I spent years getting upset over his sharpness, it gets you nowhere except red faced. But it was the day before our BE day and I was feeling violently ill with nerves. I was scared again, really bloody scared.

I got everything loaded and the pony plaited the night before, ready for our 6.30am time to leave on Sunday. All was well, and we went to the pub for a 'last glass' - much like the last supper, only I couldn't stomach food! We got home around 10 to the bloody electric having ran out... I mean FFS, what f*cking day and age do we live in!! We have a key meter, yep, you heard it! A key that you take to a shop and top up with whatever spare change you have lurking!! Only Daddy Carrot forgot to do this and on bank holiday it meant at least £100 worth of meat and fish in my freezer was going in the bin and I couldn't have a shower or find anything by candle light!! GAH!! Not ideal at all.

Our 5.30am alarm sounded and off we set! Loaded and on the road by 6.30am. The journey was swift and straight with barely any traffic. We pulled in at a Londis (lucky it had a monster car park) and bought some cigs and supplies before arriving to walk the courses and use the poo facilities. Which I did... thrice!!

The course looked ok, apart from the biggest, scariest corner I've ever seen!! Bloody crapper jacks... I'm going to ACTUALLY die at this jump, that's it. We barely heard any of the first 20 get round without penalty which only added to my terror! Show jumping looked fine, it was in a nice big arena, not on the usual grass field, with not too many dreaded fillers! I felt marginally less terrified now, I wanted to try and enjoy it as much as possible.

Tacked up and went down to the dressage, they were running quite a way ahead of time so after a short warm up of 15 minutes I thought "b*gger it... just enjoy it, no pressure." And enjoy it I did. I enjoyed the feeling of being capable at this level of dressage and I rode around humming a tune, smiling away. It was great. For once I didn't care about my score or trying to squeeze every last mark out of each movement. I just felt happy.

Happiness was short lived and got replaced by nerves again as I entered into the nemesis phase.... I just don't know what the bloody hell I'm doing here! But today, I felt like I almost did... it was almost a clear round too, we rolled one silly pole that's all. I felt great and functional, rather than a foetus in a sack of milk. My usual 'dead pigeon body' was lifeless no more!!! Hurrah! The training and practicing actually works!! And I'll tell you something else for nothing... (shhhhh..) the jumps at 90 actually felt quite SMALL today!!!

Back at the box we learnt that my dressage was a 29 so we were heading into the cross country phase and toward the corner of doom on a score of 33. I will always say "I wasn't bothered about the numbers, I just wanted a happy (ish) and safe day" but this was a delight to hear!

Down at the XC warm up my empty belly was churning and I really needed another visit to my green porta-friend, but with not too many to go there was no time so I warmed up and got ready for the countdown of death.

"You have one minute" F*ck do I?! What until I die?! Yep!!

Now, I bloody hate it, the start box, I HATE it.

I would love to be counted down from the lorry park, just amble through the start and the time ticks from the first jump (if and when you make it there!).

3,2,1; Out the box and a gallop to the first fence… we stormed it, he stood off the second jump a touch, so I smacked him down the shoulder! He hates a smack too, so I found myself apologising to him all the way to number 3 – 'the mushroom of much doom'... he backed right off that one as expected, I kicked for my life and we scrambled over it! 4, 5, 6, 7 fine... we were flying again, down to the corner... it had an alternative route that you could take but I wasn't going to let it get me!! I lined him up, tapped his shoulder and we bloody flew it!!!! We cleared it, but then I was heading to the next fence which I actually couldn't see through the tears of joy that were streaming down my face!!!!

Round the corner to the... Oh Cr*p! Pat clocked the water 5 strides out and put in the best spook he's done in 5 years!!! I was hanging off, literally almost straight over the top with both stirrups missing, luckily my air-vest hadn't deployed! I quickly shuffled my chubby arse back into the saddle, found my stirrups and kicked like stink! He went through the water and over the jump no bother!! Boy, that was a VERY close shave!

We sailed round the rest of the course, spooked a bit at the double of brushy ones but flying, we galloped through the finish line for another bloody clear!!!!!

Bursting with pride for my absolute bloody pleasure of a pony. He is by far the most rewarding horse I have ever ridden. We nailed it today but... By gum he makes you work for it! We did it, we did it AGAIN!!!

Washed off, pictures purchased and chips eaten, we set off home absolutely ecstatic. Another notch on the British Eventing bedpost and we are confidently and consistently getting mid-low 30 finishes!! Can you believe it, (banging the same old drum) that less than a year ago I couldn't even get the saddle done up out of fear? Now I'm actually out here doing it, I've never felt achievement so wonderful.

Thank you so much to everyone we met today, the Wimpy family is growing so much and for everyone's words of encouragement. You really are brilliant, without you I'd be nowhere near as brave. Huge thanks to my yard family who mucked out so I didn't have to, to my sponsors, and also to my wonderful husband.

Going out making memories with Pat and Daddy Carrot is just wonderful.

Love you all very much,

Vic and Pat Xxxx

With the next event at Chilham Castle already entered, it wasn't long before the sweaty palms were back out in force!

<u>♥ Thursday, April 20, 2017</u>

Dreams. Today I have struggled with motivation because of dreams. It's all a balancing act isn't it. It is hugely important to have a dream. Making dreams reality is near on impossible if all you do is dream about your dream and not act on it! ... you with me?

*So today I have been dreaming about my dream. The dream is to be writing, at home, in an office that looks out onto a field with Pat munching in it. To have a holiday booked and to have the second book ready to release. It is easy to get very wrapped up in a dream. The reality is, I still have 3 jobs, a horse to keep fit for eventing (next BE Day is a week on Sunday), a husband to keep happy and a house and mountains of washing to tend to. It makes getting my sh*t together quite challenging and leaves no time for a confidence wobble. Dreaming makes me so happy, and does motivate me a lot. But don't let dreaming take too long - chase the dream with actions, not just idle thoughts. Go BLOODY get those dreams!!!! I'm going after mine RIGHT NOW!!!!!*

I'll remind you again of how, if you want them enough, achieving your wildest dreams is bloody well achievable. It is now October and I have fulfilled the dreams that I had in April, however the old dreams I once had have now adapted and evolved. The dreams I had at 18 were just as far out of my comfort zone as the ones I had this year….

MITSUBISHI MOTORS CUP
5

81

817

493

356
CROFT CARPETS
358
Wimpy Eventer

467

754

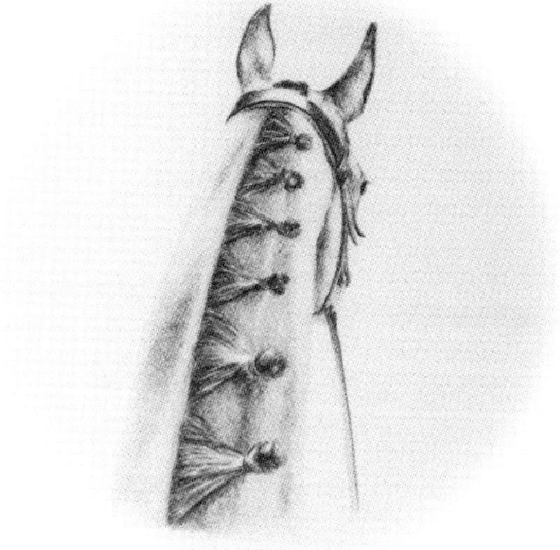

A CHANGE OF SCENERY

At 18 years old, those 'Jobs' pages of the Horse & Hound were my absolute favourite, I loved reading through the descriptions knowing that I could be very capable of fulfilling several of them, even at such a young age. I had my Pony Club B test and had been teaching in my local Pony Club at rallies all year, I enjoyed teaching kids but not enough to want to do it full time. After all, you are mostly teaching the out of breath pony club mums that are running alongside little Tabitha anyway! This wasn't for me, I wasn't yet an 'everybody's person' on the inside, I found it emotionally draining to deal with too many people all at once and pretending I was fine with it! I can act up to a crowd or a camera, no problem, but it doesn't mean on the inside I feel confident and okay about it. So, teaching was a no go, I didn't fancy dressage much either (my technical riding skills were poor!), autumn hunting didn't get going until September and I was a bit too cumbersome for exercising racehorses… But there it was, the advert that changed my twenties…

'Surrey Polo Groom Required – No previous polo experience necessary.'

In essence, I had never really left my home town much – maybe a few times as a kid, being dragged around with my brother when he played cricket for Lincolnshire. But I had no idea where Surrey was. It was February and my Dad bought me my first car for Christmas just gone. A little used Ford Ka. I had failed my first driving test after a brief brush of a cyclist who totally dramatised falling off into a ditch, so I had to pass it quick smart before I could drive the 185 miles to my interview the following week!

When you have a reason to be great and failure is not an option it's amazing what you can achieve! I passed with only 4 minor faults and with my printed off AA route planner and massive road atlas (just in case) I headed off for Surrey the next day!

My word driving on the M25 even now after 13 years of driving is a challenge, but doing it in a tiny car ALONE for the first time was frightening to say the least. I had to keep ejecting my tape from the cassette player because I couldn't concentrate with Alanis Morrissette bawling at me. I'm laughing out loud right now at how ridiculous this sounds but it felt ridiculous then too!

I got lost in the Surrey hills and had to pull over several times. I even remember having a little cry when someone beeped at me for the first time, it was all very overwhelming. My car also vibrated terribly at anything above 55 mph so it took an age to get there in the slow lane with all the lorries that I didn't dare overtake!

On arrival at the polo yard I was grilled on my experiences and past jobs, and I think I had enough of what they were looking for. The lady who interviewed me was so lovely and she would be my new teacher in this unknown field. She had tons of experience and I was very happy with the set up there. We would have 9 ponies in work at any one time, all living out so the job was mostly riding work. The male polo player and owner of the yard would come back from his home in Thailand for 4 months and play his season in that time.

Fine by me, I mean elaborate lifestyle, but like I always say; 'Aint nowt as queer as folk'!

I was offered the job and accepted there and then! I was to start in April as soon as I could, ready to start fittening up wintered out ponies…

Being the youngest of four children, the rest having flown the nest, I was making the long drive back to Lincolnshire to keep it all secret until I dared break the news to my parents. In the mean time I bought the most appropriate book to teach me about my new venture – Jilly Cooper's 'Polo'. After reading that I was fully prepared for someone with a double-barrelled surname to rough me up in the hay barn come the summer!

April came around very quickly indeed, I had my 19th birthday and a few days later realised that I still had to tell my parents where I would be disappearing to for the next 5 months! I told my mother and we agreed that she would tell Dad! He appeared very cross at first and I hated that feeling, good job it wasn't long until I could b*gger off. I know now that he would have just been worried about how I would ever get by and probably also confused as to why I would ever want to leave Lincolnshire and my home. But I did, I knew I had big things to achieve, I knew there was more for me to explore but when the day came I wasn't quite so confident!

I think I cried the whole way to the A1, which was about 40 miles! I had 'Big Ted' strapped in the passenger seat for company holding the AA map and a few new tapes ready for ejecting on the motorway! I was terrified. A few hours later though I arrived and settled in to my little bungalow at the back of the yard, and very quickly I realised how much equipment you needed to subsidise living on your own. I had to make an emergency trip to Tesco's for a bowl, plate, cutlery, a saucepan of some kind and a few weeks food shopping so I didn't have to leave the farm for a while! I'm not sure that telling my Mum at the last minute was the best idea, she'd have sorted all this out for me! But here I was, a lone ranger, doing it all on my own!

I had by now taken up smoking too, something I wish hadn't done, because now I am a total Yo-Yo smoker. I give up and then when I think I'm not coping well, I go back to the only thing that I know will relax my brain – nicotine. I absolutely DO NOT condone it and it was something I will always wish I hadn't started, but here I was on £140 per week wages and still buying a pack of Marlborough Gold because they were the 'posh' ones. The truth of it is, they all taste awful and without a Polo mint – I would rarely have a cigarette, even now!

My first day in my new job, I turned up on the yard in smart breeches, a shirt tucked in and belted, polished long boots and my best riding hat. Very quickly I felt exceptionally over dressed. My friendly teacher and another exercise rider were in bootcut ripped jeans, Doc. Martin boots and a polo helmet with a single cloth strap holding it on! I looked a prize pr*ck and that was the first and last day I wore any kind of jodhpur all summer. I raided the local charity shops on my first Monday off and soon I blended in.

Sunday nights were party nights and the JC Polo bible I had now read twice soon became reality. Polo is a very social sport with a lot of fun and encounters of the sexual kind that I fully embraced at age 19. It was short lived however because I began dating a fine young man who had years of aristocracy in his blood, just like the book! Hugo was a charming gent but with me using the word f*ck as a comma and not being able to hold my knife and fork in the right hands, I think I soon cheesed him off! It was then that I met my first husband. He was a soldier in the army which meant he was away often. This was ideal as I dedicated so much time to practicing my polo swing on the wooden horse in the evenings that I didn't have time for a boyfriend anyway!

His first tour of Iraq during my first polo season was to be the first of three in as many years. This gave us no real perception of a full time relationship. We were engaged the following year and I was none the wiser of what a 24/7 life would be like with an almost stranger.

I did learn something this year and it was the sport of polo that taught me to love speed on a horse, it gave me skills I will use even now, of stickability and riding for your life. There is no better feeling than galloping full pelt into the side of another horse trying to win the line of the ball. I was regularly covered in bruises and had used a year's supply of vet wrap bandaging up my calves under my flared jeans because trying to look good and fit in really does make you very sore. I learnt so much about the sport and even got to play mini chukkas, which isn't very common for the groom to get a go at. My boss was a great guy too and to my surprise, never once tried to lure his way into my undergarments! Darn you for misleading me Jilly Cooper… I will never forgive you!

Returning home in September and saying goodbye to my new polo friends was very sad, but the yard kept me on a retainer to come back the following year so it wasn't forever.

Going home wasn't all bad either, Lincolnshire in Autumn always makes me happy; cubbing turns into hunting, and with Christmas looming and local pub frivolity, I took a job in a little private yard to tie me over for money and of course this lead to another year of poor attendance at university!

This little yard that started as a Wednesday morning job, just mucking out and plaiting up for the lady in the house, but this was where my love of eventing really kicked in. I had the guts and horses after earning my keep with the owners. I went out and had the time of my life under a sponsor for the first time. No costs involved, just working for the family's enjoyment of seeing their horses go well.

I wasn't brilliant, I was very average, but to them I was amazing. I made them happy and brought sunshine into their home. That was the best part for me, seeing how much difference I could make to people, just getting back after a show regardless of the results and laughing at the kitchen table over a glass of wine, how happy we all were. Those memories hold a very special place in my heart and always will.

It's a funny thing when you look back and think about how massive your balls were and how often you laughed, because right now my balls are wizened prunes, they need an injection of something but I'm not entirely sure port will do the job anymore. Back at 20 years old, the jumps were never big enough, ditches were never wide enough and galloping was never fast enough! Right now, I like the idea of having Pat stuffed and standing him in my living room to hang coats from and tinsel at Christmas.

MOVING ON TOO SOON

♥ Monday, April 24, 2017

Crikey me the nerves are back!!! I have my 3rd jumping lesson with Russell tonight to try and get ready for Chilham BE90 on Saturday!! I'm scared. My last one was amazing but I was very nearly jumped off when Pat over did it at an oxer and I feel scared that it might happen again. I did feel so much more confident than this after the last session and when I jumped my round at Bovington, so maybe I'm making it up in my head again!! Either way, I have drippy palms and daren't have any lunch for fear of staining my pants later on!!

*So, my next D Day BE Day is Saturday, I am number 81 in section B at Chilham Castle. After that (providing I don't die) I was *thinking* I might do a BE100!!!!!!!!!!!!! Can you believe I just wrote that down?! Thing is, I have something to prove this year, to myself mainly. I want to prove that ANYTHING is possible. Anything you dare to dream, if you work hard enough to fight the fear. Borde Hill is meant to be a nice 100 so here is where it starts, that build up to the fill out the entry form without pooing on my desk chair in a shared office... ARGH!!!! If you do anything today, make sure it is praying for me and my survival!!*

I did of course VERY quickly scrap this idea and thought I would do what I know is a tougher BE90 to make sure we were really ready. Tweseldown is a bigger, up to height course – that'll do… but alas, someone in the eventing fate kingdom had other ideas.

♥ Tuesday, April 25, 2017

*Sh*t, P*ss and B*gger it... I meant to enter the BE90 at Tweseldown but I appear to now be running in the bloody BE100!!! I entered and then the email confirmation came through only to reveal my fatal mistake. Holy Mackerel! I've had 2 poos since I saw my name on the list!!!! Now, my lesson last night was GREAT, nothing to fear at all. I felt capable (for a change) and not like a limpet! I now need to book in some schooling at Tweseldown so I don't die of terror in advance of May 21st and also get* *to Coombelands and show jump over some bright fillers. I cannot tell you how nervous I feel right now! Focus, bloody focus I still have Chilham 90 to get my bloody boiling on Saturday. ARGGHHHHHH!*

So that was it, fate decided. I knew I could have changed it and re-entered the BE90 but I thought in my head, if I did I would almost certainly die. I am a firm believer in fate, wrongly or rightly and because of that it meant that my meaty BE90 was now a meaty BE100. I will be my own failing one of these days. All the focus back to Chilham Castle now and having a super confident run out for us both.

♥ Friday, April 28, 2017

It's Friday... the times are out for tomorrow's D Day. BE Day at Chilham Castle - 11am, 12pm and 12.30pm. There are a few things I would just like to clear up before I go any further;

*Number 1: I have just had to have a second poo and do you know something...? It's DRESSAGE related!!! To my horror the test is bloody AWFUL. There is no free walk, the canters are around the arena not on a circle, there are so many mentions of the word diagonal... P*ss flaps! Free walk is my redeemer, my point scoring movement! I just watched someone's test on YouTube and I needed a poo. What is happening to me?!*

Number 2: I am getting used to sweating profusely and can thoroughly recommend Dove cream deodorant. Whilst no industrial strength product would stop my dripping pits, this at least masks the smell of level 5 terror, with the soapy scent of a 1980's launderette.

So here we are, Friday again. What a week. I want to talk about passion, it's very relevant for me right now, I have realised over the last few months that without passion, you know that fire in your belly, the burning desire to want something more than you ever have, well without it what you have is - 'Half-Arse-itus'. It's curable but you don't want it, trust me.

You might have days where you just don't want to live life anymore, you don't want to get on and ride, you feel intimidated by everything and everyone - I have been there, I have felt those things, and I promise with everything I have that it isn't forever. It doesn't have to be like that. You are so bloody wonderful and you don't even see it, every single one of you deserves to feel like you CAN do ANYTHING you dream of (Well..Maybe not flying, flying might not end well, let's leave that for birds).

*What I am saying is, feel passionate about something and things will start happening whether you like it or not - magnetism, gravity, fate, who know which one but something makes that sh*t happen! Get that fire in your belly...*

I'm off to take my own advice and NAIL IT at Chilham Castle!!

EVENT REPORT – Chilham Castle BE90

Chilham BE90 – The One with the CLEAR ROUND

So, this morning's 6.30am alarm wasn't even needed, I was already on toilet trip number 2 by 6.00am. The balls I grew yesterday (and all week in fact) had shrivelled away to an unrecognisable size and I was SH*TTING MYSELF!!!!

We loaded and left by 7.15am and arrived at Chilham at 9.30. The course walk was so b*starding hilly... Christ! I need to give up smoking! I didn't hate any part of the course in particular, I just wasn't keen on the barrels at 2 nor the jump that was far too close to the water!! But I was hyperventilating by then so I was just glad to have made it around the course on foot without pooing myself or fainting!

Tacked up and walked to the dressage. Pat was testing my patience this morning, I was so scared. I had run through my dressage on the back of a receipt in the pub the previous night and felt terribly unprepared. Who doesn't ride the bloody test through at home?! Me apparently!! I was scared, nervous, trying to hold my poo in and the tw*t tries to bronch me off. I wanted to go home there and then.

Now the BE97 dressage test is a b*gger. It goes down the centre line and where you would usually go all the way to C in front of the judge and turn, this turn was at X!! I forgot and made it to G before I remembered …FFS!!!! P*ss poor planning!

I was so cross with myself and came out thinking it deserved a 36% ish. I came back to the box unhappy with how scared I was of riding again. I could have cried.

Onto the jumping, we didn't have long, I watched a few go and decided I wanted to buy a shovel from the tack stand and dig myself a hole to hide in. The arena was surrounded by banners advertising certain fatality, flapping flags of death and there were far too many fillers to get over. I swallowed the bile down and got on board, warmed up and went in!!!!! Two lessons with the godlike creature that is Russell Cooper in the last few weeks meant we used the new skills we had been taught and we were sailing over the last fence CLEAR!!!! Bloody clear!!! I sobbed into his mane wailing with joy!! F*cking clear!!!!!!!!!! Get in my boy!!!!!

The death phase.... no pressure, running on my dressage score. I couldn't remember the course, but in the nick of time, as I got counted down I got my act together. 5,4,3,2,1..... bloody go go go!!! 1 and 2 jumped lovely, he was flying... 3 on an angle that I totally screwed up, Pat chipped in, wrapped the fence hard and twisted in mid-air. I so very nearly fell off, hanging on by the skin of my b*stard teeth again!!! 5,6 jumped lovely, almost approached 7 from the wrong direction but we made it, legged it down the row 8,9, 10 was a house and step down which he boldly took me into. (Now I will add that Pat isn't a brave XC horse and I sobbed all the way down the hill to the water because for the first time HE took ME to a fence!!!!!).

Waters x2 rode lovely, another steep gallop up hill to the home straight, where some lovely Wimpy supporters were cheering us on! Ping and ping over the double of houses and down to the train to finish. We sailed home 13 secs inside the time!!!!!!!

A double clear, finishing on my poorly prepared dressage score of 32 meant we placed third!!!!! Bloody 3rd AND picked up our Badminton Regional Final ticket!!!!!! I cannot tell you what this means to us, to everyone involved. I am so bloody ordinary and so is Pat. I just wanted to do my best and do it well today. I wish I had practiced my test because only one point separated us from the top spot, but who gives a sh*t!! We are doing it, me and my beautiful boy. He truly scared me in the dressage warm up, but what a feeling on the XC, it made up for all of the fear.

Daddy Carrot learnt to do studs today too... result!!! He's so bloody supportive, not sure what our outings would look like without him by our sides. Thank you so, so much to everyone supporting us in every context, you make this worth it, this rosette belongs to you.

I love you all.

Goodnight and God bless Love, as always

Vic and Pat Xxxxxx

So there it was, the best possible outcome we could have hoped for, before we move up a level. It didn't make me feel any better though. 100 is such a big number. It's not just the height or technicality of the fences, it's the different calibre of people you get attending the 100 days. The 90 days are usually run on the same day as the BE80 and those people are out and out amateurs, this is what we are and this is where we are happiest. At BE100 you are likely to be in the warm up with a professional on a younger horse, or people that really know what they're doing. This frightens me more than ever. I never really feel like I know what I'm doing and I don't need reminding!

We had a couple of weeks before we had to face our fears so I thought we'd better at least get round a course of 100cm show jumps first. We headed to our local venue of Coombelands for a bash at the 90 and the 100.

EVENT REPORT – Coombelands 90 & 100

So here we are, the day of doom... I arrived at the yard at 12.30pm to give Pat his 'Super so Kalm' paste that I've been trying out. It seemed to have worked, because when I came to hack my 30 minute trip to Coombelands, Pat was suitably snoozy. It didn't last long though. We arrived and scattered a few horses in the warm up with his terrifying dance moves, he knows it frightens me… why do it you knob!! I spent ten minutes learning the course and 15 minutes warming up and we were in!!!

Crikey, my heart was pounding out of my chest! I royally ballsed it up, by fence 5 I had 2 down because the little b*gger was spooking at EVERYTHING!! My nerves had crippled me and I left him long and cr*p to nearly every fence. I had one more down and left the arena absolutely terrified about having to go back in when they were bigger!!

The 100 coursewalk scared the living sh*t out of me. I hadn't realised that the timed section could include fences at 105cms and as 100 was already the biggest course we have EVER jumped I was seriously considering pulling out. Three withdrawals on the board didn't make me feel any better either. Daddy Carrot told me to get my act together and give it a go, even if I have to retire at number 2!! Deal!

I warmed up and he didn't feel that confident over a meter oxer in the warm up and nor did I!!! 5 to go, I watched a few, learnt the course a bit better and then it was my turn! I went in and gave it EVERYTHING I had, it showed! Jumps 1-6 were a meter and 6-11 were 1.05, he was flying. Upright, Oxer, Double... nothing felt too much for this little horse today. He was soaring. We had a very unlucky roll of one pole, but with only two clears in quite a big class, I was VERY happy with that (and to not have died!!!).

The placings were announced and Master Patrick was read out in 3rd!!!! The fastest four faulter!!! I couldn't believe my ears, I sobbed a little before collecting our rosette, prize money and Sunshine Tour qualifier!!! I gave it my all and truly felt deserving of that good round and frilly token. We hacked home in the sunshine and felt on top of the world - and I still do - we jumped a bloody meter course and didn't die!!! I didn't want to go at all today but look at us. My darling boy has done it again!

STRAIGHT TO THE POINT

Here it is, the part where no matter how rubbish you're feeling, you need to sit up and listen to this bit.

I want you all to realise that above all else, f*cking things up is actually perfectly fine. I've royally f*cked up a lot of things in my 31 years and I've survived and bounced back stronger than ever.

Something that is absolutely pivotal in aiding confidence for those riding, competing, tobogganing, etc. is knowing that it is ABSOLUTELY 100% FINE TO F*CK IT UP... if you don't die, you can only learn from it. Seriously, the chances of you dying are so very slim, you have almost as much chance of dying having sex or popping to Tesco to get your Imodium.

Anything less than death is just a learning curve. It's fine to have a stop XC or fall off in the dressage, it is okay to soil your pants in the warm up, it really is. People might laugh, but b*llocks to them, Captain Karma will soil their pants much worse one day and hopefully in public! There are times where you need to take the pressure off and stop worrying about the 'what if' moments that give you palpitations. What if you don't die? What if you take something from each experience, something you can work on and improve. Focus on making the negative 'what ifs' into positive ones.

If you take the pressure off and focus on keeping the experience as a jolly good time ... really, there is nothing to lose. Christ... I have no dignity left so b*gger it, let's be aving' you!!!

You need to get this mentality ingrained into your skull, I have it most of the time now and it makes for a much less pressurised life where you can actually start enjoying rather than fearing.

If only I had this experience earlier on in my non-horsey side of life! At 21 I wasn't massively outgoing, I didn't have the knowledge I have now or the ability to step away from a situation like that. I got married at 21. I got married knowing it was probably not the most sensible thing to do, but I didn't stop it happening. At the time I was totally swept up in planning the wedding, my fiancé was away a lot and we still hadn't lived together yet.

I b*ggered up my last few exams at university and whilst my dissertation received a First, I technically didn't graduate – something I don't regret now but I did for years. It frustrates me now that I didn't stick at it… but that was me all over back then!

I remember feeling worried the last few weeks before the wedding, I didn't eat much and my dress was then too big. I dropped to 8st something and I'm not particularly small framed. I had a niggle, a seed of doubt that unbeknown to me, would grow into the biggest and most aggressive tree of cr*p you ever did see! It wasn't great from the outset and without a job or mates I grew lonely and massively lacked confidence.

I look back now and think about the person I was back then, I was away from my family, the people that know you best, I wasn't charismatic, or funny very often like I used to be at home larking about with my brother. I didn't really know who I was or where my place was. My husband was much older than me too and so were the people we socialised with. I remember being at an Army function and in the loo, over heard two other wives talking about me and how they didn't want to socialise with someone their daughters age, I felt sad after this. It was confirmation that I wasn't really ever going to fit.

We fought a lot my husband and I, usually over how much he drank and things escalated into a situation I wanted to get out of quicker than a fire in a kindling factory.

It wasn't all cr*p though, I made a very good friend in this time too, one that I will cherish for all eternity and for her home that I ran to frequently for comfort.

That brings me on to something VITAL. Friendship. Shut your eyes for a second and think of one or maybe two people that you really consider a lifelong friend. I have one in particular that stands out above anyone else and I think, always will. She and I have been there for each other in our darkest times, we have seen each other at our most stripped bare (Quite literally when she had to be cut out of her jodhpurs after a horrid fall!) and without judgement, we have picked up each other's broken pieces more than once. But just think about how much that keeps you going, even if you don't speak often or see each other every week just knowing you have someone that 'gets you' is really very important indeed.

I love being that person for people. I know there are so many people that need that helping hand and I know how much this means. Even now, when I went and did my last event of the season, she was replying to my confidence wobble text at 5.30am – we are 250 miles apart now, but it doesn't matter one jot. These are the ones, the ones we talked about before in the first book. How important it is to surround yourself with people that don't give a sh*t, ones that would give their last sh*t to see you succeed or ones that don't know what sh*t you're doing! I do think though they are the first people to tell you when they think you've gone totally insane and stepping up to BE100 still being nervous as hell at 80 deserved a telling!

The week running up to my first 100 was exhausting, my body was trying to fight off the worst flu I'd had in years. I was on my knees with hardly any energy left for riding and practicing. I remember trying to have a lesson and poor Russell having to cut it short because I was struggling to get my breath. This was not boding well for the weekends challenge!

By the time the day arrived to walk the course, I felt no fear at all. I had no adrenalin left in my body that wasn't being used to fight the virus so I slept soundly for the first time ever the night before an event.

EVENT REPORT – Tweseldown BE100

So here it is... our first BE100 report.

I would like to start by saying (for anyone that is a new follower or an old one that might not know), up until July 2016 I was unable to tack up this dear little horse without sweating profusely. I was scared of riding to the point of fibbing to cover it up. I didn't hack, I certainly didn't jump and I would lunge for at least two days before I braved a 10 minute sweating session in the school.

Today marked our 6th BE event **ever** including the two at the end of last year. We have done 1 at 80, 4 at 90 and this one - our first 100!!!! I'm pushing my limits, with the energy I have left after this blasted virus; I'm terrified and I'm certainly not afraid to admit it.

So here goes... Our 5.45am alarm call to leave the yard at 6.30am hit me like a train. I have been riddled with flu all week, feverish, snot ridden and unable to breathe if doing more than sitting... today was no different. I felt foul.

At the yard, a small panic soon resolved by my beloved Husband Daddy Carrot of unsticking the lorry door – I was hoping it was stuck fast for a minute and we could just go back home instead! Alas, we loaded my Patsy and trundled off on our 1hour20 trip to Tweseldown. Now for some reason, I don't like the venue. I feel it is so beautifully and professionally presented now, that I find it all a little bit intimidating. I meant to enter it to face my demons and complete my last BE90 before stepping up... well I entered the wrong bloody class and fate kept me from amending my error!!!

Walking the course yesterday, I felt nothing but ill!!! I wasn't overly nervous because I met a lovely old friend on the course that guided us around and shared her knowledge, which helped us a lot. They were however MUCH bigger than they looked in photos online!!! No offence to Daddy Carrot but his course walking comments usually consist of 'that looks a bit big' and 'are you sure that's in your class?!' So, a helping hand was very lovely.

Back to the day itself... We arrived at Tweseldown, gave Pat his calmer in a bit of breakfast and went to check in. I was number 467 today, I do prefer even numbers if I'm honest!

I got ready and we warmed up, he wasn't silly, he was in fact the best he's ever been in the warm up!!!! AND this continued into the test!! It went lovely, I was struggling to breathe at times but he was soft and round and didn't gawk at anything too obviously!!! We pulled it out the bag for a 29.5 brilliant at this level, I really was very happy with that!

Not much time to get ready and jump because I had yet to learn the course! I put his boots on and b*ggered off down to the show jumping. Now, this is only the second 1m course we have ever jumped so it was still a bit of the unknown. He warmed up super and over jumped all the practice fences like a stag! I went in and had to be reminded that my bell had gone!!! Bloody flu makes your ears feel like you're underwater sometimes. And there it was, my ring paralysis again… The b*stard spooked and jinked in front of every bloody jump!!! He made me work for every stride as he was clearly TERRIFIED of fillers and poles again!! The reality of this is, that I was probably SO tense he thought he had something to worry about. He launched at number 3, two strides out and landed splat on the back rail and then had an unlucky rub of another, but by the end I was exhausted…my God did I ride for my life?!

Hand on heart, I don't think I could have done any more. 8 faults to add and we were lying in 9th place going XC!!!!

So here's the thing. I left the show jumping ring and felt like a 30 stone fat bloke was sitting on my rib cage. I couldn't breathe, snot was pouring out of my face and I just *had* to get my hat off, my head was thumping. I was still not nervous and this worried me more than nerves. I worked it out with my very basic science, that all of my energy and adrenaline was fighting infection and not making me nervous. But don't you need adrenaline to focus?! Quite right you do.

For 20 minutes I seriously toyed with withdrawing us from the cross country. Daddy Carrot didn't really know what to say, he knows how much it means to me to not let people down or myself and so I half heartedly said I would get ready, warm up and then decide.

Down in the warm up I felt committed... there was no turning back now, we were 4th on the board and very quickly I was in the start box (of doom) being counted down!!! 5,4,3,2...1!!!! Let's av' it... snot drenched or otherwise- we were off!!!!!

I galloped out and got a crap jump at number 1, a very kind hanging log, but Pat wasn't paying attention and it all felt horrible. I slapped him on the shoulder as a Perky McPerk and because I knew if something didn't get better, we'd never make it round!!! Number 2 was a house, he stood off a little but we had a better shot at it, up the hill to 3; a log pile, it was bigger and probably the biggest XC jump we had encountered (yet)! He sailed it, on the angle to 4 which was partially hidden by a tree. Of course he spooked, but we scraped over it!! A long gallop up the hill to the WATER!! The hanging log that I was sh*tting my knickers about yesterday jumped lovely actually, straight in the water and out at our first attempt over 6 - the dreaded Captain Quackerson (shaped to look like a duck)- WE BLOODY JUMPED IT!!! First time too!! Now I will add that I thought it was highly likely that we'd have been eliminated at one of these two jumps, so hadn't really planned for how I would feel about the rest!!

Anyway, I found my missing stirrup, thanks to the over excitement at the Quacker and off we went!! 7 was bloody massive, a big trailer but it jumped lovely, 8 a bloody great table on a down hill line which didn't look too friendly. He soared through the air and gave me the most wonderful jump over that, I could barely get my breath, but I yelled 'bloody good boy' at the top of my lungs!!! It felt awesome!!! 9 a log thingy, was very trappy and wide but hitting a bounding stride, Pat made nothing of it!!! 10 - the second water... with a jump into it!! We've never jumped into water but I thought we'd have a bash!! He hopped the log and splashed in and out of the house no bother!!!!

Down the long galloping straight to a big ask at 11, a huge table coming off the corner. Daddy Carrot didn't like that one yesterday so I kicked and grabbed the mane extra tight and we sailed it!!!! 12 the open trakehner, he didn't even look at and then onto to 13 - oh 13 you b*stard!!!! 13 was a hanging log to a skinny triple brush... I flew in over the log, didn't really look, or take a pull or do anything much and Pat got confused and ran out the side. I of course just sat there like a dead f*cking pigeon!!! We re-presented and I slapped him down the shoulder right on take-off, he sh*t himself and jumped through the b*stard flag!!!! For F*cks sake!!! 2 refusals at one fence is costly, a 3rd is the long road home... so I trotted at it, full up 1.05m brush and he popped it from a trot like it was a sodding cavaletti!!!!

Tit!! Vic you are a total tit!!! The poor horse didn't understand the question, he was poorly guided and I take full responsibility for those 60 penalties. We put it behind us and bounded on... 14, the angled brushes actually jumped very well, 15 a log pile also sailed nicely and over the scary dragon to finish!!! Now I know on paper that when our 9th place and rosette turned into a 3 figure score, most people would feel a bit cruddy but it was the BEST F*CKING RIDE OF MY LIFE!!!!!!

We did it, we survived, we came home smiling and full of running. My bloody beautiful boy, he sailed all of those massive jumps like they were nothing, he galloped across the course just eating up the ground for breakfast. It's not about the prizes for us, it's about our trust in each other, growing that bit more with every round, the love I have for this horse is incredible.

Thank you all so, so much for the words of kindness and 'good lucks' thank you also to the commentator who by all accounts and despite having no course notes, talked about the book and about Pat and I as if we were so special. It means so much to know there are so many people that care about us. I'm dosing up and snuggling with the cats and Daddy Carrot for the evening now.

What a bloody great day!!

Love as always Vic and Pat Xxxx

Just reading that back now, I am sobbing. Sadly (and you'll see why in the next chapter), they aren't tears of joy, but tears of what could have been. I'm disappointed in myself for the next series of events and how I dealt with them. I will NEVER let that happen again as long as I am sucking air into my lungs.

DON'T LET PEOPLE NEAR YOUR CHIPS

The exhilaration of the weekend's event lasted for days, I didn't feel at all beaten by our misunderstanding at fence 13. I felt empowered and I knew we could do another one. I did have to strike whilst the iron was still hot though, because I know if I leave it for the feeling of elation to retreat… I won't do it! Whilst the blood is still pumping, I always get the next one entered… I still do this even now!

I entered my second 100, somewhere that was supposed to be much more forgiving than Tweseldown and VERY local to me. It was also going to be the very last event I did in the south of the country as we had found a house up north, Gary had found a job and our move to Lincolnshire was imminent.

My heart has always belonged to Lincolnshire. It really makes my blood turn hot when people say it's full of in-breds and flat fen land. I have no cousins that married one another, and I've seen at least two hills in the north of Lincolnshire! My first wedding was in our local church in the village I grew up in, but that was the very last day I would spend in the county before we moved 180 miles south to an Army posting. I was sad, I could tell my Mum was sad that I was going too. But 6 years later, telling my parents that my marriage had broken down and was irreparable was far, far worse than this day.

The disappointment I felt in myself for finally throwing in the towel on something you vowed would be forever, was a real blow to my pride. But, I couldn't have carried on any longer, I was desperately unhappy, scared and although it feels so cliché, I had nothing left of myself. I was sad so often, I felt as though there was nothing to look forward to and dreaded my husband coming home. At 25, that is no way to live. Wrongly or rightly I had put Pat on part livery and I had left our marital home and Monday to Friday I rented a room from a lovely couple who have turned out to also be life long friends.

Renting this room was the best thing I have ever done for myself. It changed EVERYTHING. The day I moved in there I was terrified, I had no idea who these people were but I had bought a numnah off her on Facebook so I knew she was probably alright! It was brilliant from the start, they made me feel so welcome and having told them the real reasons for the move, they helped me so much to get back to laughing again.

We drank wine most evenings and Suzi taught me to cook, we laughed all the time and I started running and doing things for myself again. I felt empowered and although I was racking up a nice bit of debt, I decided to get Pat back on DIY livery locally and then things would be perfect. They really were. I filed for divorce too, something else I had dreaded. But I did it and it wasn't so bad. I had a good job, great friends, my lovely boy back home on DIY livery and I was me. I was happy for the first time in 5 years, properly happy. It's these people, the special ones you keep in your basket along the way that make your life complete.

And here we are, 2017 leaving all of these wonderful people behind to move back to Lincolnshire, God I could cry at how much I miss those times but I am so glad they happened. And new adventures are upon us now, I think I'm ready…

The fortnight before my next BE100 at Rackham, we got the horribly sad news that my much loved Auntie had passed away, not poorly, not even old, just gone. I had made it to 31 without having anyone close to me die and I didn't take the news all that well. It's a very personal thing, grief and I wasn't sure I could carry on with my plans to do Rackham or in fact anything else, I felt emotionally drained. But in the midst of it all, I had an awful group of people that put everything in perspective for me. In a morning I had banned more people from the Wimpy Facebook page than I had in its existence. By all accounts, there exists a few closed groups of people in our equestrian community that think it's utterly hilarious to make fun of others. To criticize their riding, how they look after their horses and their integrity as people. Cyber bullying, I think they call it. This hit me just at the wrong time. With the news of my Auntie and the build up to moving again, I just couldn't deal with it at all.

For the first time in a long time, I was in that dark place of depression and unable to get out, my heart was racing leaving the house, I felt like I couldn't do anything for fear of someone telling me that I was doing it wrong. I am crying now just reliving what I allowed those nasty, horrible women to do to me. I was so glad I was moving in the end so I didn't have to bump into them, no one would know where I was. I ended up on an ECG machine in A&E after 3 days of crippling irregular heart rate. I'll point out right now, I am tough… I am not a sniffling wallflower, but this was very personal and hit me hard.

It took a few days for me to pick my sorry arse up and not allow them to get to me. My Auntie would have been cross with me for letting them ruin my fun, so I put all of my efforts into enjoying my last event in Sussex but sadly it wasn't to be…

♥ Saturday, June 17, 2017 at 5:18pm

Just to let you all know in case anyone gets wind, Pat and I have withdrawn from the Cross country today. He is safe and well. But the heat massively got the better of him and it was 100% the right decision. We made a few little rookie errors in our dressage for a 32 which left us in 8th but then he was flat as a pancake in the show jumping, chipping in a short stride into almost everything... very unlike my big jumping boy. I knew he wasn't feeling good and his needs absolutely always come first.

Very sad to be at home not having blasted round the course but there's years ahead of us yet. I want to thank you all for being there for us, for wishing us luck and making it all worth it.

Now despite that being the event report I submitted to the blog, it was in fact a lie. The heat was very unforgiving but the truth is, I bottled it. I was crippled with nerves in the show jumping warm up and ended up riding next to Tina Cook of all people, which did not help! I went in the ring and left him totally wrong to nearly everything and had 4 fences down. My lovely friends had offered to drive us there so I kept a brave face on it until I got home and then sobbed my heart out over how far back we had gone in the confidence stakes. I was right back to the beginning, I wanted to sell him. I wanted to give up and I couldn't face it anymore.

♥ Tuesday, June 20, 2017

I just want to let you all in on something that I am personally struggling with right now. I can't write this quickly and it is quite likely that it will be at least 11 by the time I have held back my tears enough to write it all down (it's now 8.15!).

For anyone that hasn't read the book yet or seen the misery, depression and times of darkness I have been through, you will all just see the exterior of what is now a braver and more confident rider. Being on the TV and blog and shown as a smiley and seemingly capable rider will have portrayed someone that doesn't look 'wimpy' at all. The truth is, my horse has now had 3 days off after attempting my second BE 100 at Rackham on Saturday, I am dreading riding him again. I withdrew after the Show jumping and I was relieved that I had the soaring temperatures as an excuse. The truth is, I wasn't mentally capable of going around that course - there I said it. I was back to feeling frightened and whilst I had a cry over the disappointment, I was crying tears of feeling 5 steps behind where I have been the last couple of weeks.

*I am crying about it again now - I had come so far and I feel like a f*cking failure again. I really do take so much from the support that is offered on here and try desperately hard to ignore the occasional negativity.*

It's a funny thing, confidence. Some days I feel up for jumping big jumps and then other days I can just about fill his water buckets. Your personal life plays a huge part in this, and mine is extremely up in limbo at the moment. I feel desperately low again and it isn't something that will go away over night. I guess the point is, bare with me, that I will be back and fighting the confidence fight very soon but in the meantime I won't be entering anything like what I had planned to.

I don't want to feel like this and I need time to work it out. I'm sorry for pouring this out but I felt as though I needed to remind myself that it is okay to feel like you are failing sometimes. It's ok to not progress all the time, it's ok to sob your heart out in frustration over why you can't do it when it seems everyone else can.

I dearly love you all and I thank you once again for supporting Pat and I through this journey.

Love as always xxx

It's so sad to think that just one small blip like this and I'm broken, back to square one. It was hard to pick myself up after this, but we had a house move to contend with and it was 200 miles, a house, the cats and the pony to move! Amazingly, we are incredibly resourceful as a couple and got it done in 3 days!!! We spent the week before boxing everything up and then hired a van and a horse box and did it in 4 runs up the country!

The night we loaded the furniture van was one of the oddest feelings. I had already done my goodbyes at the yard and so most of my tears were cried, but finally when we loaded up and headed off to the pub for one last drink, we realised there was NOTHING left out of the van. There was not even a pillow or duvet! We slept on a mattress under a sheet and had the worst night's sleep you could have got, ready for the long drive and unpack the other end! It was a pretty emotional day!!!

3 days later we were unpacked, it already felt like home and I was fully embracing a NEW START.

It's the only way sometimes, when you hit rock bottom. It didn't mean that I wasn't still getting wind of the mean things people were saying about me, but I was learning to ignore them a bit more and I actually find now that I would rather not know what's being said. I am actually very nice as far as humans go and I would never, ever want to make someone feel bad about themselves. It's just a shame that not everyone feels like that. I took a piece of my own advice and decided to mentally f*ck them off in my head. No one that says nasty things about me deserves my energy and worry. NO ONE. The one thing I have gained though, is one of those nasty b*stards was saying how much my hands moved and they were right… I've worked really hard to make that better, just a shame I think of their snidey comment each time I feel my arms wobble!!

The bottom line is, those that mind don't matter and those that matter don't mind. The people that I love and who love me; they are supportive, they are encouraging, and they are worth one hundred of every single one of the Chip P*ssers!

Bugger off my chips with your stinky p*ss, there's nothing for you here! And there it was, 2 weeks into moving and we were BACK IN THE GAME, albeit 80cms, but I had entered an unaffiliated one day event.

Wimpy Eventer
THROSTLE NEST SADDLERY
3

467

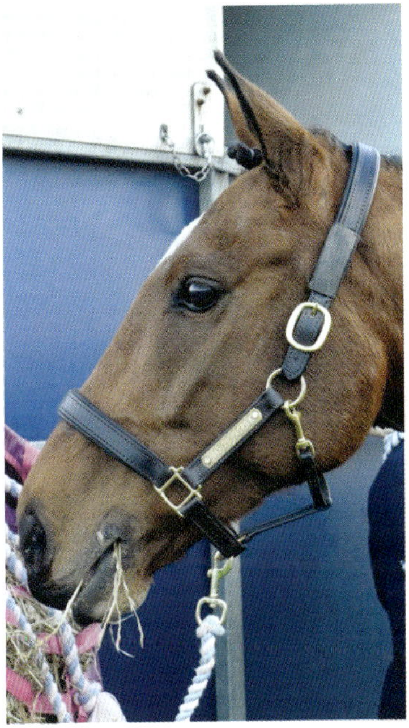

BACK ON TRACK

So moving back home to Lincolnshire is something I have dreamed of for over 7 years now. I am not quite sure why I stayed in the south for so long, because unless you can afford monstrous rent, you are forced to live in towns, sacrificing garden space for marginally higher salaries. You can get just as good a job up here though (as Daddy Carrot has proven) and the rent is at least 30% less in most areas!

Now having secured work for us both and finally unpacked all of our boxes in the new house, real life commenced! Only it was different now. I wasn't getting up and rushing around every morning, or dicing with daylight hours to fit in a ride. I was far more at ease and the palpitations that had landed me in hospital had finally subsided. We booked an actual holiday too!! What a treat!

I was exhausted though, the last few months had really taken their toll. First and foremost you should take care of your body and your mind, I hadn't done this and it was letting me know!! Mental health is something I have always found a bit taboo to talk about, until now.

In the past I have been naïve enough to think that anyone one with a mental health problem needs a royal kick up the arse. People wallowing in self pity. I now know that this is bullsh*t. It was my way of trying to cope with the way I felt at the time, sad, lonely and probably suffering myself.

Chemical imbalances in the brain, grief, stress, pain, guilt, worry, fear, anxiety; any one of those can result in depression if it consumes you enough. We shouldn't be ashamed of that. EVER. I am taking a bloody stand right now. I have been scared, I have felt fear, I have been consumed by worry and stress to the point where I cannot think ahead of that day or even hour without feeling overwhelmed. It's more common than you think and it is NOTHING to be ashamed of.

I'm still susceptible to it now, I just recognise what it is, and in my own way I deal with things that are getting to me and move forward. I don't just brush it off anymore or box it away and like I said in the very beginning; you must deal with things in order to move forward without them coming back to bite you in the arse.

I have now accepted that it's ok not to feel or act happy all of the time, it's absolutely okay to feel scared and vulnerable, and my word is it perfectly normal to want to curl up under a blanket and sob your eyes out on occasions. I know that's ok now, it's perfectly normal, so I just need to find things to break that sad cycle.

The most important thing for me is to be around people that understand in the same way I do, those things right there. If someone comes along and tells me to 'cheer up', OH! Expect a punch in the chin my son! That is the single, worst possible thing to say, listen up fellas... NEVER say "cheer up" if someone looks sad. It just makes you feel like you are the biggest sloppiest fun sponge, sucking the life out of everyone! All it takes is my husband to wrap his arms around me and tell me that I am wonderful to him, that's all that really matters. If you don't have a husband, that's fine too – a cuddle from your cat or dog, a drink with a good friend, a hug from your mum – they will all help because you ARE WONDERFUL TO THEM too. Surround yourself with positive and caring people that get you. And tell them how you feel, tell yourself too, don't try and hide it and pretend to be happy, it might work for a while but it won't long term. Fake smiles are easy to detect when you start smiling real ones that burst with joy, remember that.

I won't rest until people, particularly in our little Wimpy community know that they are safe, that it's ok to feel not ok and that you will never ever be judged unfairly. It's up there with animal cruelty for me now – and I will never, ever take for granted my mental health for as long as I am breathing.

While I'm on the topic, if you know you have said something to someone lately that might have made them feel sad, or was intended to make someone feel inferior because you happen to think you're better… Come on now! Don't be a chip p*sser. You really have no idea how your words might affect someone who battles with low self esteem or depression. Yes, they might have come across a bit of a d*ck but you really never know what is going on underneath. It could affect them for days or years even, so be kind, be mindful of other people. Remember that everyone has a story to tell. It's much better for your own mental health to live a life never judging or keeping score. Putting other people's feelings first will make you feel fulfilled in a way no chocolate bar or glass of wine ever can.

With this in mind, and after some of the negativity I had faced of late, I was back to the frequent toilet visits and white knuckle fear of show days, the week leading up to my next event. I had entered the 80cms and it was nice and local, so no rushing about to leave 4 hours ahead of my times. Now my saving grace was that whilst a group of people that didn't know me from Adam were being hideously cruel on the internet, I was lucky enough to have met the most wonderful people that were our new neighbours. Two of these people we share our yard with and happen to be the biggest hearted people I have ever met and ones that I hope we are friends with for a very long time to come. Auntie Smurph and Grain Pirate Dan.

These people have restored my faith in humans, they would NEVER judge me and without realising it, they have turned around my whole season this year.

EVENT REPORT – Hackthorn Hall ODE 80

Burton Hunt Pony Club ODE – HACKTHORN 80cms

So today I *might* have sneaked off and done an event without telling hardly anyone!!!! I was having a HUGE wobble in confidence and with time off to move I was worried I wouldn't be able to get back out there and do it again! So I entered the 80-85 Burton Hunt Pony Club - Hackthorn ODE on our first wedding anniversary no less!!! I've been frequenting the toilet all week trying to learn the test!! But walking the course yesterday I felt at ease with the height and decided it was a day of absolutely no pressure.

We arrived courtesy of a taxi from our lovely new yard friends Auntie Smurph and Grain Pirate Dan, and that's when it hit me. I'm actually far more terrified of getting on to even warm up than of the competition. I had no pressure to perform but I was still sure I was going to die getting on him!! I need to deal with this, but today is not the day!

The three musketeers (Pat, Daddy Carrot and I) headed off to the dressage where he warmed up very nicely and actually did an ok test. I made a couple of mistakes and didn't feel that he was listening at times but I thought it deserved a 31 or somewhere near.

A little wait until the jumping, so I actually walked the course (which I NEVER do, it makes me so scared actually going up to them!!) and I felt surprisingly not too bad. There were less fillers than I had expected which is great for my spooky beast. The jumps were a maximum height of 85cms which I was very glad of, I could just go and have a nice time. And a nice time we had!!

A sterling (if a little low flying) display from the RAF Red Arrows overhead and we were off... very nicely over all of them just a little spook off the corner at 6 for four faults! I was VERY happy with this.

Back at the box we were melting!!! It was so terribly hot. But on we got and off we went. Everyone at the event was so wonderfully friendly, even the counter downer in the start box of doom didn't scare me today!!

We set off and tripped over fence one a little log, over two and three, the house. Sailed the big table at 4 and the hanging log over the ditch at 5. We galloped over 6 and 7 a log/ditch/log combination and up the hill over a big fat log at the top. The ground was exceptionally undulating and hard work for my Patsy but he made nothing of 8,9,10 or 11 until we stumbled into the corner at 12 and he fell face first onto it! A little scratch on the neck and a check he was okay and he popped it no bother the second time round! Over the scary blue pipes at 13 and down to a big joker fence, a 95cm palisade (that had an alternative), I grabbed the strap and kicked and he soared through the air and galloped away like it was nothing, I felt bloody wonderful after that. Over the log, the mural painted double and down onto the water where he made nothing of a big jump in! Out and over the last, he sailed through the flags grinning just as much as me!!

What a horse, what a day and what a feeling!! I'm buzzing!!! I can't wait for the next one... my horse and me, we are on fire again!!! I popped back to grab my sheet and a picture (or 6!!) and it actually turns out that with a dressage of 23.8!!!!!!!!!! And one pole down and 20 to add for our face plant XC... he came 6th and we got a lovely rosette!!!

I cannot thank everyone at the Burton Pony Club enough for being so welcoming, supportive and well organised. I love Lincolnshire and being local to home at an event was just so nice today.

I had a lovely, lovely day and now I shall enjoy a little gin and tonic with my husband on our first wedding anniversary.

Love as always

Vic and Pat xxxxxx

We had such a good day at Hackthorn, and dropping back a few levels was just what we needed to get back into the swing of things. At the time of entering I felt a bit ashamed of doing a lower class but now I've done it, I have realised there is no shame in taking the pressure off. It was the best decision for us both. It was no good going out scared at a level I can just about manage and frighten my lovely horse. Sadly, this nice feeling was a little short lived as the online bullying after this event got ten times worse. I didn't post on the blog for almost a week because yet again I had let people drag me down to that horrid sad place. But this time I wasn't going to let it break me.

♥ Monday, July 17, 2017

*I want to talk about something that has been playing on my mind the last fortnight, something I haven't really felt confident to say out loud. I know I have been quiet, I haven't felt confident to write or publish anything much because of the negativity I have experienced from some serial chip p*ssers. That's not because I feel 'caught out' for being a fraud or that I have run out of things to 'make up' to tell people... (ROLLS EYES), I have been deep in thought, trying hard to take my own advice in times of uncertainty.*

I have been doubting my ability as a rider - yes my hands are wobbling about, yes I am unbalanced and yes I am hanging on to my poor horse for grim death at times - I do not profess to be a professional by any stretch, I have mountains to learn and take criticism well! But when the criticism is just nastiness, I struggle to make light of things. It all stems from the tiniest seed of doubt, but that seed is enough to rock the biggest boat in the stillest ocean.

*I mean COME ON... don't you dare let them p*ss on your chips! DON'T YOU BLOODY DARE!*

Our sport of equestrianism has enough challenges, we do not need other people making it harder. Why do they do it? Why does anyone feel the need to make another human being feel so desperately inferior?! I know this is usually because of their own lack of self-belief, but it's just not on! Yes, I am no longer crying at the thought of getting on my horse, I CAN jump a jump, gallop in an open field and enter a show, does that mean I haven't overcome some huge hurdles to be able to do that? I still feel the fear, I just bloody well do it regardless.

I'm sick of feeling guilty for progressing and this is me taking a bloody stand! I know that I am never going to feel 100% confident even at 80cms, but if I can do it anyway and show the world I can, then it makes it so much more accessible for others - why is this so wrong? - I'll tell you - IT'S NOT!!!

For anyone that is going through any kind of negativity, don't you dare let them beat you down, focus on what you know is true, take comfort from those people that believe in you and stick two fingers up at the ones that don't.

Seriously - every single bloody one of you has something to be proud of, don't you dare feel ashamed for that. Celebrate it, make something for yourself and be bloody proud of it. I am not hiding behind my low confidence anymore!! Here's to the sun shining and to all of us feeling damn well good enough!!! <3

Love as always Vic and Pat xxxxx

I wrote this post not really knowing if I believed myself 100% but after it being the farthest-reaching post I have ever done with hundreds of stories and pictures of other people feeling proud of themselves, I knew I was right in my thoughts. This touched over 297,000 people – that one little post. B*llocks to anyone that says I'm a sh*t rider, I am – there, I agree but I'm a nice human and if I make life easier for just one other person I will carry on doing this, badly or otherwise!

And that was it, with my new house, my wonderful husband, my own business, good, supportive friends around me and my dear sweet Pat, I waved my sharpest middle finger at those serial chip p*ssing b*astards and got myself back out there! I entered Frickley Park BE90, my first affiliated event up here and YES, I was still frightened!

♥ Wednesday, July 26, 2017

And so it begins!! The damp palms, the profuse sweating, the palpitations and increased toilet visits.... it can only mean ONE thing!!!! WE'RE GOING EVENTING. Sunday is D-Day BE Day for us! Hopefully early enough times to not scare us silly! It's been a while since my fluff up at Rackham, we had a good spin at Hackthorn unaffiliated but it doesn't stop me feeling like my insides are doing the Macarena! I'm going to learn the test today and practice tonight and tomorrow in the fields on our ride, we have a jumping lesson Friday night and a good hack Saturday before the big day!! Here goes nothing!!!!

The funny thing about fear is that for days on end it has me feeling utterly dreadful, even on the day all I want to do is pull out, but afterwards it melts away into the biggest sack of joy you have EVER experienced and makes all the bitten nails and toilet visits SO worth it.

EVENT REPORT – Frickley Park BE90

So here it is....

Pat, Daddy Carrot and I headed to Frickley Park today for the BE90. Yesterday's course walk left me feeling oddly excited to get back out and doing this sport again, I felt 75% excitement and only 25% terror after walking the somewhat boggy going of the XC course.

After walking the course we went to Auntie Smurph and Grain Pirate Dan's house for another #westfirsbycrew BBQ (did I mention, I love where we live) and played a game of rude scrabble until much later than planned!! Although I did stumble upon the brilliant and newly created word 'fungina' that I now plan to include into my vocabulary. Although, this meant that silly Vic drank half a bottle of Malbec and felt like an utter 'un-fungina' when the alarm went off at 4.45AM!!!

Carrot drove us to get my pony and we loaded up and left! I felt SICK. Not just because of the hangover but because I just wanted to turn around and go home. Crippling nerves got to me big time today. I felt fine yesterday, well not fine but nearly fine.

I almost cried on the drive there and again when we sat in the queue of lorries waiting to be TOWED IN!!!! Yep! I was severely close to tears now and all I could see were people skidding about in the show jumping arena out of the passenger window. It was awful, I couldn't get out and run to the porta-friend quick enough!!!

We registered, got my Patsy ready and I hopped on, as close to the box as I could so I didn't get too muddy. Walking down to the dressage warm up without my gel bum sticker-inner always makes my heart palpitations come back with a vengeance, today was no different. I have been using a gel seat saver that grips you on for over a year now and I feel lost without it! A lovely lady Wimpy follower stopped us for a chat but (I'm so sorry) I was a dreadful wreck. We went in to the arena and smiled our smiles, we did everything where we were meant to and it felt bloody amazing!!! I wailed to pat what a good boy he was and gave him a big squeeze!

I was so proud right there, I would have happily retired after that!!!

A short 30 minute change over and we were in the show jumping. It was my worst nightmare of tonnes of spooky fillers, slippery mud and mountains of on lookers, this combination resulted in me riding like a total turd and thoroughly deserving 2 poles down!!!!

Another half an hour passed and there we were, deep breathing our way around the XC warm up. Now at this point, silly Carrot had said we had the best dressage in our section!!!! And with 8 to add, we were 6th place and couldn't be pipped to this spot unless I failed him XC... I think after 2 stops at Tweseldown, not even making it to the XC at Rackham and the stumble at Hackthorn as my last 3 outings, it was safe to say I was rock bottom in my belief that I could still do this.

I felt weak, unfit and not sure which fence I would just plop off at... but we were there doing it, bloody doing it regardless of how green I was. I won't let my nerves get the bloody better of me!!! "Get in that start box of doom you great big fanny!!!"

"3,2,1" came quicker than expected and we were off!!! Galloping!!! Flying the brush at 1, the wall and roll top for 2 and 3, sailed over the double of bullfinches at 4 to a gappy hedge at 5, I was squealing with excitement now. It felt bloody awesome to be back there in that moment with my horse. 6, a flower dressed table caused Pat to back right off but I was there to catch him just like he does me when I'm scared, I kicked and yelled to him it was okay and he flew it and then boinged off the step down the hill!!

7 a house, 8 the trakehner and 9 a shot gun cartridge all jumped lovely! 10... the first worry for me, a skinny log into the woods and a couple of strides to a second one... I don't know why I doubted that trusting little soldier today, he flew them both and out the other side like I was daft to assume otherwise!!! Another hedge and a wall led us to the water which he splashed through no bother, then onto my doom fence!! We all have one, the one you are most likely to die at... 14 was it!! A big bright CORNER!! I lined him up, slowed him down, showed him the question and he answered it perfectly... bloody boing!!

Over we were... just like that!!!! Down to a flower box, wagon and the home straight of a wall and sacks to finish!!!!

Aaarghhhhhh!!! We did it!!!! Bloody bloody did it!!! My horse is a stonking legend!!!!! We did it! Clear!! The sad part is that because I was cautious of the mud and him slipping over, we went a little bit steady and did ourselves out of the frillies... but... bugger me, we bloody did it!!! We CAN do it.

Today I love my horse, I love my Daddy Carrot and my will to make this work. I won't let fear determine who I am... not on your life!! And I won't let anyone else define who I am, me and my horse – we were brilliant today.

Thank for the endless support and encouragement, I love you all.

Love as always Vic and Pat Xxxxxx

With another round under our belts at an unknown venue and after a few weeks of emotional upset put to bed, I felt ready to fight again. I can and I will!

TWO STEPS FORWARD, TEN STEPS BACK

I started my 2017 eventing season in April and we are now 5 months in with only 3 months left… look at everything that has happened in this time, the first book flew out the door from May onwards and I am delighted to report it has been very well received – I am now writing about the reception of a book in the sequel book, not knowing how this will be received… RISKY!! But, I was exceptionally worried. I am no J.K Rowling, I didn't even study English past 16 years old! (sorry about the bad grammar!) But just that small confirmation that the content was helping so many people was enough to make my heart soar, what a feeling. With each message of thanks, I still well up now, it is a very special feeling being a game changer for people and long may it continue.

♥ Wednesday, August 2, 2017

Some of the lines from my first book (especially the 'things to remember' pages at the back) are really resonating with me today. I cannot begin to tell you how much I want other people to succeed, to progress and to love who they are. Today is Wednesday, it's raining again and I woke up without my Carrot (he's in the big smoke today). I instantly felt flat. So I started the thought process that I go through when I feel like this.

*Firstly, I allow myself to wallow - I think this is important, it's ok to feel sh*t, it's okay to think of all the things that are negative in your life, things that you would change if you could.* THERE... RIGHT THERE... *'If you* COULD*' - Well you bloody well can, so step two (after wallowing in self pity) is - How do I change it? The only way you can begin to change a bad situation or feeling is to suffocate it with positivity. Change your thought process from how crap you feel about something to 'what do I have to be grateful for?' or 'how can I make an impact on things today?' Take your mind away from things you don't have, things you can't do or things that leave you feeling like a sack of mouldy pears and start dwelling on the things you* CAN *do.*

I started then to dwell on the reasons I am happy and the things I can improve on, that started a fire in my belly instantly!! I want to change the *world, even if it is just my tiny piece of it, so that's what I am bloody well doing!! I'm not sitting there going over and over in my head, the things I can't do as well as I'd like, I'm focusing on the things I feel good about doing. They might only be small things - I make a mean poached eggs on toast, so I started there - see, small things but they came out perfectly and I felt better!! The bottom line is - divert your negative thoughts like a wasp heading for your wine glass, waft them away and sip your delicious wine... There will always be wasps - deal with it! Squash out those negatives with big fat positive thoughts! You've got this nailed, you just might not know it yet. Have a great day <3 xxxx*

And so with positive thoughts in mind and a burning fire in my belly, I entered my next event another unaffiliated one, we are doing the 90cm One Day Event at Epworth Equestrian. As we got a 3rd place at Chilham Castle earlier this year, it qualified us to enter a Regional Final. If you come in the top section of riders in this qualifying class you are on your merry way to the much coveted slot at the Mitsubishi Motors Cup held at Badminton. This event is run over the same week as the world class Horse Trials, so we were desperately in need another confident run before our first ever Regional Final in two weeks!

EVENT REPORT – Epworth 90

Well, today was a mission of two things. Number 1 was a confidence boost before our regional final in two weeks and Number 2 was to get inside the time after being told my horse didn't make the time at Frickley because he was FAT!! I was even more determined to do it!

Now walking the course yesterday (alone!!!) massively put the jitters up me. I thought it looked big and beastly and there were three skinny ones that I was worrying my beans about!! The show jumping also looked big and bright! Tomorrow was going to be the first event of my whole season that Daddy Carrot would not be coming with us. It was tough to get my head around but the events keep falling on football match days and I have to be fair. Today Auntie Smurph was our taxi and friendly helper to replace my Carrot and this was the next best thing.

We had nice early times and pootled down to the dressage for our time of 8.30ish! In the warm up he was very subdued and in fact he was a little lazy. A novelty compared to the spooky monkey I usually have to deal with! In the arena, I thought it rode well, it was the same test I did at a Frickley and I definitely felt today's wasn't as good but no mistakes and no shooting off. Big pats for not spooking and back to the box.

A quick tack change and off we went to jump... only to find out it was causing cricket scores!!! Great! I am still not 100% confident that I will ever learn how to ride my horse in the show jumping. He can be a different horse from one half of the course to the other, but we will always give it our best shot! I warmed up swiftly, not too many practice jumps but no waiting about before going in either (my new tactics, thanks to Daddy Carrot observations!) I thought about what Carrot would have said "take your bloody time" don't rush to the first jump. My Carrot isn't horsey, he has just seen me bugger it up enough times now. So with him in mind I didn't rush, I presented to every jump and kept the canter consistent...It worked....WE BLOODY WENT CLEAR!!! And I had heard the dressage score too... 26.3!!!

Now normally we are clawing at a placing by now but not this time, we had nailed it... lying in FIRST PLACE by quite a way too, we were heading cross country... I was nervous that I would let him down at those skinnies, so I rode positively from the off. Charging into practice jumps like I meant business! There was no one waiting to go so I went and asked if I could, I did and cantered straight through the start box of doom without having to endure the dreaded "3,2,1"!!!! I kicked like stink from the off, the house at 1 jumped lovely, around the corner and a short gallop to a sneaky turn that didn't show 2 in sight until you were on top of it, Pat dropped the anchors on like a hot coal... I knew he would do this, I've had a similar thing before at the water at Bovington so I was ready for the brakes to hit and I was there with a bum smack and a yip yip and he sailed it!!!

Out into the open for a nicely attacked number 3 and into the woods again for the first ask of the course. A barrel, over a mound and out over a skinny brush (my demon jump) well not today my friends... no sir-ee!!! I lined him up and locked him on and we flew it! On to a line of jumps at 5, a narrow trakehner at 6 and a roll top and coffin at 7, they all rode very nicely indeed! Number 8 he backed off, it was a big hay cart with shavings bales in front, but he flew it with a big kick from mum! 9 was my let up fence, nice and plain, 10 the water was a jump in over a boat and out over a wishing well skinny for 11. He jumped it all very confidently indeed! 12 I was crying over last night, a big brush with a ditch in front... I kicked and shut my eyes and he did stand off it quite a way, but we made it!! Phew!! Down to the castle for 13, round the corner and over the bridge, which left you down hill sailing over the flower box at 14. We didn't get the best jump at it but we made it over! 15 the Carrot box jumped great, to 16 the skinny I was fretting over... no bother, I set him up and slowed it all down and he popped over like a dream. Bobbed down the step afterwards like a pro.

Then it came, I was out of breath, long in the rein, relieved to have got over all the ones I was worried about and what happened.... the f*cking cone of doom happened!!!! It hit us, right where it hurt! A single road cone at the side of the fence and his heart fell out his mouth. He backed right off and ran as far away from the doom as he could!!! I swiftly turned it into a loop and growled like a goodun' and he flew it!!! 18, 19 and 20 down the home straight all galloped lovely!! And that was that!!!! First place fell way down the swanny as the spook and loop at fence 17 hit us with 20 penalties to add!

Now there are very important things to take from today, never to get complacency when any kind of obstacle of doom lies before us, never to change the way you ride for the results you have already achieved and never under estimate the power of positive riding. I don't feel sad about losing first place, we achieved both of our objectives today and I feel on top of the world. It was a big course and we jumped clear in our nemesis phase. I feel very, very proud indeed. I'm not sure where we ended up but who gives a badger's ass... my horse was a bloody legend today!!!! Thank you to my lovely Auntie Smurph who drove us there today and was so mega supportive. I think we both had a soggy eyeball moment when I came out the show jumping!! Love him so, so much, I don't ever want this feeling to end.

Love as always

Vic and Pat xxxx

So we survived another outing, our first one without Daddy Carrot too!! I felt a little bit deflated as it would have been our first win, if I hadn't have ridden like a total sack of cr*p but the fact that I had just done another 90 after weeks of worrying I couldn't carry on… I was feeling good. And this was just a warm up for what was set to be the most important event of our year; our Badminton Regional Final (only a week away!).

Now I well and truly succumbed to the pressure of this event. I had built it up SO much in my head I couldn't think about anything else. I rarely get like this but the emotional highs and lows of the whole season were all a surprise to me. I took Pat cross country schooling in the run up to this event, something I rarely do and I'll explain why…

The feeling that you get on the day of an event is like no other, you cannot replicate it. I have a mental block in my head about the way I ride the cross country on the day that I just cannot put into practice at home. When I get in the start box on the day of an event, I give it everything I have, I ride every fence with passion and I feel invincible in that moment. Why else have I got that ridiculous smile on my face the WHOLE way around? I'll tell you why, partial insanity but total sheer elation!!! But, when I try and jump a log on a cross country course for practice… I feel like I want to cry. I feel scared, I over analyse everything, I don't ride forwards enough and this results in a terrible confidence knock for us both. And although you might see videos of Pat and I storming around the course like our pants are on fire, Pat is NOT confident AT ALL. I have to seriously work for every jump sometimes from 10 strides out!! If I could bare it, I would love for someone else to ride him round, just to see how much you have to do to coax him over each jump. Luckily he is more scared of doing the wrong thing than of the jumps so as long as you get the right balance of pressure to praise, he'll jump the moon for you… we've got each other sussed now I think.

I probably should add in at this point, that I do vaguely know what I am doing. Although it might not seem like it at times! I have ridden some fantastic horses and trained with some brilliant people over the last 25 years and I know I have 'feel' which is often something people lack and struggle to learn, so when someone comes along bashing me for not going XC schooling – I know that not going is the best thing for ME and MY horse.

I have done it a handful of times with and without a trainer and each time I have felt it has lessened our confidence. You must do what is right for YOU in this life not what society tells you is right. Christ, there are 4* horses that can't go cross country schooling and some that even have to do fittening work in the arena because they won't hack… you tell me I'm wrong when the world's best do it their way!!!

If you judge your suitability for eventing on a bad cross country training session, there would probably be no need for these grass roots levels. Give it a go I say, and ride for your life on the day! As long as you are safe and not totally out of control, it's the only way you'll know for sure if you love it or not.

Right where was I…?

The day of the course walk (Saturday), Daddy Carrot and I had a HUGE falling out, because we rarely argue it always seems worse than it actually is. I was being totally selfish, stubborn and neglectful of his feelings. I let this event take over my life and I was outraged that he wasn't being as supportive as I had demanded!! It's awful really when I look back. I bet a lot of people reading this have snapped more than once at their non-horsey partners the night before a show – it's human nature but I really wasn't very becoming! In fact, I feel ridiculously sad about the whole weekend when I look back, which is a real shame. I will NEVER ever let something that is meant to be a FUN hobby affect my marriage EVER again. It is absolutely not important enough for that. I regret being hideous to him and I hate that I can't take it back. I think it was Karma, the way the day of my one and only shot at a Regional Final panned out.

EVENT REPORT – Shelford 90RF

So here it is.... my long awaited Regional Final at Shelford.

I had been working hard all week preparing as best I can for this day. I went XC schooling for the first time all year, jumped him in the field and practiced my test. I was getting horribly nervous and putting stupid amounts of pressure on us to be the best we can be for 14 minutes of judged performance.

Carrot and I walked the course on Saturday which because of bad traffic, took way longer than planned – queue me getting increasingly ratty by the second!! There wasn't anything there that I was terribly worried about and not too many plant pots or fillers in the show jumping either!! RESULT!

Now, honesty is the best policy, so here it is... I was so desperately wrapped up in this stress and pressure that I failed to be anywhere near a decent wife and quite rightly my Carrot was getting increasingly peeved over my stress and inattentive, selfish behaviour. We had a very rare argument on Saturday which wasn't helped by my transport mix up and having to drive miles to get another lorry!! It was fair to say that this event took over my life. Something I will never ever let happen ever again!

I was on at 8.30 so I had to leave at 5.45am. Still stewing from our argument, I left my Carrot sleeping and thought 'F*ck it, I've got this, I'm going for it on my own!!!' NOTE: actually TOTALLY ALONE I didn't know anyone going either!!!

I arrived at the venue of Shelford, a very lovely unassuming place that is only an hour away. I got my number, notified the secretary of my lone trip and headed for the green porta-friend to relieve my terrified bowel. I got my Patsy off the box and tacked up. Now, normally I have to get someone to feed him while I get on because I terrified of that! But I have been trying a new syringe calmer by Blue Chip Feed and it meant he just stood there at the water barrel while I scrabbled on!! I was so happy right there, it's the little things and what a long way we have come that make this journey ever so rewarding. One of my biggest fears is getting on at a show, today I put a lot of those demons to bed.

He warmed up without any tension or sillies... I couldn't believe it, I felt safe and happy and gaining confidence. Then who should arrive, my Carrot with his camera. I have to say, I was so happy just having got on by myself that I didn't give two hoots about our silly row anymore!

Into the test, and I thought it was okay, nice and accurate and everything where it should be. I have felt better tests but I thought it was due around a 28 comparing with my other tests this season.

A quick change and into the show jumping, I have a new tactic in the jumping that I am still working out but it is getting so much better already. He is so sensitive, spooky and then racing about that it's hard to get a balanced and consistent canter round a course. I tend to hook him up and cripple the canter so today, just like my clear round at Epworth, I let it bum twitchingly bowl forward!!! It worked again!! One silly duff stride at number 6 was all the wobbled us for 4 faults!!!! I was over the moon!!!

I was perplexed however, to hear my dressage score was 35!!!!!!! What the actual fig!! Bull sh*t did I deserve that hammering, he did a sweet test and I rode very accurately indeed. My marks were lost because his mouth was open, that my canter transitions were abrupt and my halt 'drifted slightly' - it is the worst mark he has EVER had EVER and it certainly didn't feel like the worst test, by a long way. I know it's all relative and everyone else in the section was marked hard too, but it left us right down the leader board and definitely not going to Badminton. At this point, I was so bloody thrilled with being able to get on by myself that I didn't give two sh*ts about the score and decided we were just going out to enjoy the rest, so we went to get changed and have a cuddle before the cross country.

He warmed up well and in 15 minutes we were being counted down!! I screamed with joy out of the start box, YIP YIP and over the first, I gave him a little left-handed shoulder tickle with the whip as a gentle reminder that darting to the left isn't going to work today, he sailed over the palisade at 2. He flew round the corner for a giant leap at a hedge at 3, I slipped my reins and squeaked with terror as I was left shocked to the core again, he NEVER takes over but he gave it his biggest hairy balls over that hedge!! Galloped down to a ladder at 4 and up and down a dip in the woods and out over a big log for 5!!

He was FLYING, no hesitation, as soon as I kicked and shouted 'go' oh boy, he went! 6, 7 round the corner to a shavings bale filled table at 8, hit a perfect stride for that and sailed it!! Pinged the yellow pipes at 9 and back into the woods for a sticky jump over a log for 10, hopped off the step no problem and galloped down to another big log for 11. 12 was a ditch/step up with 4 strides to a hedge, he bloody nailed it. Hopped up, perfect stride and flew the hedge like a lion! Down to a huge beer barrel clad wagon, hit another booming forward stride and soared through the air, I squealed again, this time in sheer delight, this was possibly the very best he's gone, ever... galloped over a steeplechase brush with tears of pride stinging my eyeballs ....DONT GET COMPLACENT VIC, YOU RETARD! Focus!!!

Down at the sloppy, murky water, he splashed in and out and over the roll top no bother and screamed down the home straight to the last fence... we soared it, we did it!! We bloody well did it. Ahhh, you just can't put into words, tears are beading down my face right now, I had the best round of my life yesterday. He was unreal, like never before. I couldn't have given less of a cr*p about not going to Badminton, I was and still am over the moon with the whole day.

So we did it again, me and my tiny boy. He is just my dream come true, it has taken all my effort, confidence and patience to get him here but together, we've done it again! In any other section he'd have earned a rosette to finish inside the time today.

Now I said it would be a long post today.... You may have noticed a brand new logo attached to my saddle pad this weekend. I am absolutely delighted to announce that I have been selected to represent FALPRO as a sponsored rider!!! Pat has been wearing the rugs for a few weeks now and I cannot tell you how brilliant they are... I will go into more detail about which ones I love the most, but I seriously cannot thank them enough. I know we will do them proud after today.

One last thing... Yesterday was also magical for another reason. We welcomed our beautiful new boy into the family. 7 year old Bentley joined us yesterday from Cheveral House Racehorse Rehoming run by the lovely Kate, who we will continue to support for the rest of the year. She works so hard to find the very best homes for these lovely horses and I couldn't be more thrilled with our lovely boy. Watch this VERY exciting space.

So, what a day, I hope everyone takes a second to squeeze their ponies today, to reflect on how much happiness these animals can bring us, regardless of the endless heartache and fears, they are just wonderful.

Love as always

Vic and Pat xxxxx

And there it was, all the stress and heartache of trying to qualify was all over in just 4 minutes of dressage that the judge didn't like today! It's madness. No Badminton Grassroots for us, but then there's always next year. The season is very nearly over, I have a handful of runs left so I thought what better way to ensure I never get a rest this winter…. ANOTHER HORSE!!

Enter Sir Bentley, or Bender as we have now stable named him, he was about to be 'Feral Beryl' but luckily for him Bender stuck! Get an ex-racehorse they said, it'll be fun they said… Well this is not the first one for me, dear sweet Sparky was the first, then India after that and a couple of the polo ponies we picked up for those two seasons I did, they were off the track too so I knew what I was getting myself in to. I had asked the lovely man that owns our yard if there was room to double my herd and he agreed. That was that. 2 days later I was off to pick him up.

I hadn't had to look far for my Bender as my beloved childhood teacher and guru had recently picked up a horse from a lovely place not too far from us; Cheveral Racehorse Rehoming. I was worried about not being suitable enough for their criteria, I know lots of people want these horses when their photos get released online so I wasn't getting my hopes up too high. As soon as I met him I knew I would love that horse until his dying day, I think that the lady could see that and so I was therefore very suitable indeed.

Now buying anything that is described £750 'unridden' in the details, isn't going to be ready for Badminton next week and I was fully prepared to play the long game. This particular horse had been turned out in a field for a year after his unsuccessful racing career ended in 2015. He was ready for a job!

The day I fetched him was the same day we missed out on our Regional Final, I was rather annoyed to be doing it alone but as Daddy Carrot was still a bit miffed about our argument, he went clay pigeon shooting with Grain Pirate Dan instead! Not ideal, I had no idea how well he travelled and yet again I was in an unfamiliar hired lorry. He loaded a little reluctantly but didn't move an inch all the way home!! I was worried on a few occasions, when I took a corner a bit sharper than I should have, but still without movement, that he might be dead or escaped!! But no, I got home and dropped the ramp and the poor love was WET THROUGH. He was clearly shell shocked about the whole thing and was sweating profusely… much like I do these days too, but he was very much alive and well!

I let him off in the field with Pat and they were friends instantly. This was wonderful to see, Pat is a proper bottom feeder in any herd so I was glad Bender seemed a nice sort. 3 days later I attempted to bring him onto the yard, oh the stress and panic that ensued! He was NOT HAPPY about being anywhere alone. That's ok, its early days. I grabbed Pat to stand with him and all was well in the world.

A few days later we started long reining him. This is a process that means you walk miles with the horse attached to long lengths of rope in front of you. You do this usually because you are too scared to mount them and feel it safer to accumulate 60 blisters walking miles instead! But 2 weeks of long reining and he was very pleasant indeed. We have had a few altercations regarding who goes first when being led (the human or the horse) and who stands on whose toes. But he is a very quick learner and didn't need telling too many times.

My advice to anyone thinking of getting an ex-racehorse is that if you don't have the patience to complete a rubix cube wearing a blindfold, forget it! You have to be kind, firm, patient and regardless of any goal, dream or milestone you might have planned for that day/month/year, you MUST be prepared to fail and move on to something else.

They are rewarding, they are clever, they have a busy brain and like a job. They also have the heart of a lion and if you win over a thoroughbred, they will give you so much joy you won't know what to do with yourself.

Some of the earliest days with Bender I sat at home in tears. I had forgotten what producing horses was like and how unforgiving it can be when 5 days of no progress other than backward steps leave you feeling empty. How no-one tells you how much you'll appreciate just a moment of calm where things go how you wanted them to.

I lunged in the p*ssing rain one Thursday afternoon trying to get him to walk nicely and just stand without spinning in on me… nearly 40 minutes of walking around a field soaked through to my knickers… and for what? A f*cking halt!!!! FFS! But that's the soggy type of endless patience it takes because now he does it on the button.

Now, in the past I have got on board long before this point because I have been royally fed up of walking everywhere! But Daddy Carrot has been very involved with Bender when the nights were still light enough and has been learning how to long rein, and pointing out all the time that 'there's no rush'. He's right, the minute you rush is the minute it takes you five times as long! I had leaned over him in the yard a few times and he was very calm, he doesn't fidget when he is saddled up at all. We practiced standing at the mounting block for 10 minute stints every day for a week, being feed nuggets at the block, patted at the block, watched the human jump up and down at the block! Which meant that when the human finally put her tiny foot in the stirrup and got on, standing at the block was a piece of cake! He stood like a statue, I walked forward a few meters, gave him a big pat and got off!!! Secretly very relieved to not be dumped on the hardstanding!!

I know it's probably ideal to be getting on in an enclosed space with a soft landing but the joys of having the horses so close to home means that we don't have the luxury of an arena. And quite honestly, you don't NEED one, it's just nice to have. For years I feared hacking and field riding and now that's the only option, I am nowhere near as scared. I'm learning to just get on with it. I used to dread tacking up and going down to the school just as much, now I just bobble about in my homemade arena in the field!

It might appear sometimes, that other people have far great chances of success than you because of what they have. Material possessions and a wonderful indoor school won't get you anywhere without hard work. They might be successful on their own merit and luck might have graced them with those things. My beautiful new saddle won't make me great over night, and yes I am very grateful for the support of Voltaire Design, but I will work harder than ever to make sure I do them proud. That is what makes success.

♥ Friday, August 4, 2017

Here's something to think about today. Sometimes you might look at someone else's life or what they have with envy or resentment without really knowing anything about that person. Sometimes people tell you things about a person that may make your opinion or judgement of them swayed in one direction or another.

Negativity is a violent and horrible thing that, if you let it can spread like a virus and eat away at your whole life. Do you know how much happier the world would be if everyone was kind and encouraging and people eliminated negativity? I have been thinking a lot about this lately and what I can do to make a difference. I want to breed kindness, inspiration and positivity. I want to make people feel good about themselves because it makes my life feel worthwhile. Do you know how wonderful it feels to make someone happy? To say something kind and make their eyes light up. To tell someone they ride beautifully, that their horse is a credit to them, that they look lovely today... Mean it and say it or keep quiet - IT REALLY IS THAT SIMPLE!!!

Words have the power to lead, to inspire, to build up and equally to break someone into a thousand pieces, choose your words with love not bitterness. We are all human and we all feel emotion, wouldn't it be brilliant if this industry was known for its support network rather than its rivalry.

Today, I want you to tell someone; your mum, your mate, your husband, your farrier, your post man - ANYONE, tell them they are great, that they are doing a good job, give them a reason to feel happy. Be kind and spread that kindness as far as you can. And do me a favour.... Before you do that - Go look in the mirror again (one hand on the boob, if you will) and tell yourself first - because YOU ARE BLOODY BRILLIANT, you are great and you ARE DOING A GOOD JOB. You are! Believe it and spread it, do it now. Xxx

One of the nicest things about putting yourself out there in full view for all to see is that you get to help make a difference to the lives of so many people. In the last year I have lost count of how many people this Wimpy Wonderland has helped be a little bit braver or a little bit happier. It is all down to spreading kindness. I know the things I think in my brain will help other people because I know that they would help me if I read them. I have bad days and just writing down advice that I would give myself actually helps those days get better. Kindness is a wonderful thing that we all have at our disposal, why not use it more often? There's no charge and the rewards are wonderful.

So, we are coming dangerously close to the end of the Eventing calendar and if I am brutally honest, I shall be glad of a rest. The stress, the worry, the battle with nerves is really getting hard now that I am tired from 9 months keeping my fear demons at bay. I was actually not dreading this next event as much as some of the others. I think because I had been to the venue before, I knew where everything was. It really makes a difference if you are worrying about getting on. We were going back to Frickley Park for another bash round the BE90.

EVENT REPORT – Frickley Park 2 BE90

So here it is... Another soggy day in Yorkshire.

All week I had felt very at ease about this one, I think after the pressure of my Regional Final at Shelford, I had made a conscious decision to not allow this Eventing lark to ruin my mood or my marriage!!! I have a new regime the week running up to an event now, which appears to be working. I must do 3 things in order to not die/enjoy the event day as much as possible:

1. Take him out somewhere, anywhere! This week we went to a dressage clinic for our new riding club. Getting him out with others means he isn't such a dork when I'm frightened getting on at a show.

2. Give him enough work and don't be lazy! I usually find an excuse to prevent riding everyday but as long as he's done something the day before with maybe a couple of rest days early in the week, it makes for a much calmer boy!

3. Jump! I don't like show jumping, I doubt I ever will, but I have put a jump up in the field and I just make sure that the day before I have jumped it a couple of times (Jeez Louise it's barely a 2ft crosspole!!) - but, I think it makes it less of a shock when we get to the event and have to jump 30+ jumps.

So, with my routine nailed, I went off to walk the course Friday afternoon ...ALONE!!! I'm getting good at this alone time… I'm definitely not as scared to do things by myself anymore which is progress in itself. I was done in half an hour and had decided that I wasn't getting beyond fence 13 so I may as well just go and enjoy and expensive combined training!!!!

Fence 13 was a big double of very skinny logs on a curve, I wasn't ever getting him over them in my head and had admitted defeat there and then, some things will never change eh?!

Home, ridden, plaited and packed up for our 5am start, we headed to the pub for one!! One turned into two glasses of Shiraz on an empty stomach followed by a take away curry and a later bedtime than ideal! Why do I do it, what a bloody idiot!!!! I woke up nervous at 4.45am and feeling like a cardamom seed was implanted in my throat, I couldn't eat and despite brushing my teeth, all I could taste was Indian food! NEVER EVER AGAN!! I felt dreadful, sat on the toilet for 10 minutes, toying with pulling out altogether but instead, I hauled my stupid arse out the door and we arrived at Frickley at 7am!

My dressage was at 8.12 so we had time to get registered and spend a bit of time in my green poo-box of salvation!!! Yet again poor Frickley wasn't blessed with sunshine, it was bloody teaming down with rain too!!

Now, here's something else to note. I have had some bad experiences getting on at shows and I HATE it, I mean, I fear it more than waking up with a beard of bees... I think I might have mentioned this before… I've been trying out the new calmer syringes from Blue Chip Feed. I usually think these things are just a fad and filled with squirty cream, but they have changed everything for me. I give him 10-15ml of the 30ml syringe and leave him for half an hour. He is a dream after that. It's our 'miracle squirts' and it makes show days so much less tense.

He was a total angel in the warm up AGAIN!!! I can't believe it, I was actually having to kick him, such a nice feeling when usually he runs from my leg and frightens the pants off me. He did a lovely test but as I feared, we got the hard marking judge we had at Shelford!!! Compared to our other tests this year I'd have said it deserved around a 26-28% but alas, we were on a 31.8 but in the top ten of the section on dressage score so I wasn't displeased.

A quick boot up and we headed for the phase of disaster, the make or break for us. Our show jumping scores have ranged from one down to four down and with only two clear rounds all season, I am starting to think show jumping hates me! He's a big b*ggery b*stard is that Mr Showjumping. He regularly makes me feel inadequate and useless! I hate him as much as he hates me!!! But Pat warmed up beautifully with a small break in proceedings when a poor lady had a nasty fall coming into the oxer. Poor love, I hope she's not too sore this morning. It wasn't long before out turn, and in we go...

He barely spooked today!! It was a miracle!! I've started leaving it to him a bit more and it's working!!!! Normally I hook him up or push too much or just generally get in the way, but he's usually spooking and then racing in equal measures! Not today! Just a brush over the planks at number 8 and he came out with just 4 faults!!! I feel like it's getting so much better when you have rounds like that, I'm so looking forward to getting my new jumping saddle now, I might take back my words of hatred!!

So, having decided that I wasn't getting past fence 13 on the course walk, we re-named cross country; the f*ck it phase!!!! A quick change and we were in the warm up swallowing bile and deep breathing. Pat was reluctant to stand in the start box today, he was jazzy and ,ordinarily, had I not have been pooing my pants over the course that lay ahead of us, I'd have probably been scared of his jazziness, but I think he's just starting to love this part a lot!!

"5...4...3...2...1"!!!! Boom, he flew out the box like a whippet!!! A short sprint to the first and he was FLYING!!! He felt so up for it today, none of his usual spook related reluctance!!! Up the slope to number 2, a palisade, he soared on a big long stride and I was beaming!! YIP YIP.. down to number 3, a roll top, he backed off it!!! What the actual fudge! It was nothing, but by Jove it made me buck my ideas up!!!

Now I was actually in the driver's seat rather than the boot of the car in a duffle bag... I rode for my life. Short reins, determined grit, number 4 the hedge oxer sailed by, 5 the box jump and drop step left us feeling confident for a long down hill gallop to a spooky White House at the bottom. I kicked and YIPPED and he soared! Wowzeroonies... what a feeling!! 7 the trakehner, was a shut your eyes and kick job and it worked a treat! 8 was a big feeder type jump and one of my let up fences, he took the bit and flew! 9a&b, two skinny logs with mushrooms in the woods, he didn't even look!!!! Just locked on and with a bum squeeze, he pinged over both and galloped down to 10, the hedge! Flew that and the same over 11 the dressed dry stone wall! Oh god! 13 was creeping up...

Into the field I was sure to be eliminated in, I had to really work hard to get him over the army tank at 12 (great start to the field of doom). Here it was, 13... I found a good line, I held it, I kept a short rein and a firm holding leg and he locked on and jumped it!!!! Sh*t the actual bed!!! Now what... turn, turn, turn, you moron!!! I did the same at part B and it bloody worked!!!! Arrrrrrgghhhhhh!!!!! Bloody YEEEEEEEAAASS!!!

Yeehaaaaaa.....

Oh buggeration... I hadn't thought much about the rest of the course! We splashed through the water and over the boat house but wait, the doom wasn't over because 15 was that awful white and green corner I hated the last time I was here! But I took the same tactic, short reins and firm leg... he went!! He bloody flew it. Then to 16 the flower box, he thought about darting out to the side but mother had turned into Mary King today and he had no chance! Boing!!!!

A long gallop down to the ornamental wall and he stretched for a big one, full of running we galloped down to the last fence and with a kick, he soared it. We flew through the finish 6 seconds INSIDE THE TIME!!!

Bloody Nora what a feeling!!! Bursting at the seams with elation and adrenalin, I sobbed. He listened to me, I rode him, I rode him well today. Probably the best I have ever ridden in my whole life and he was just unbelievably brilliant. I am utterly delighted with him, what a way we have come from that fearful little lamb I nursed around at the start of this season!! He is an absolute wonder, taking any small shred of confidence I can give him and storing it away to make the next run even better. That is why I love horses.

We finished 11th out of 43, with 0.1% holding us back from a rosette! But who gives a finger of fudge!! NOT US!!! What a horse. He is my heartbeat, my very best friend and I just adore the absolute bones of that tiny boy.

Thank you all so much for the support, as always, you are the reason I keep going, I keep pushing my limits and facing my fears. Really. Thank you. And also a huge thanks to my support team of sponsors, because I truly wouldn't be able to afford to do this sport without your help and encouragement, thank you so much for believing in someone so desperately average.

Love as always

Vic and Pat xxxxx

What a bloody run that was, I am looking forward to feeling like that more often. That is progression for me. The placings and rosettes mean nothing if it was all a fluke on the day. I was riding better, feeling more in tune with my horse and actually enjoying it more – that's all the progress I need.

Back at home, educating Bender was getting interesting too.

♥ Tuesday, September 12, 2017

So we are entering Benders third week with us. There has been a minor setback in his settling and Thursday evening I had to put him back in the field after I slapped a wet fish around his chops for ploughing through me more than once!!

He had clung to Pat and apparently as Pat left his eye line he took Benders manners with him!! We have since parted them in the field and I gave him a couple of days to let that sink in. Last night I tacked up and lunged on a huge loop in the field. He trotted over some poles too!!!! He truly redeemed himself and made my heart sing. He is getting quite a character now his slippers are on and his chair is warm. I sharn't be letting him forget his manners and become rude but I do want to earn the trust and respect of my new love.

There is a VERY small margin for error here and you need to be able to re-adjust the plan in the blink of an eye without feeling disheartened. Firm and fair is my tact and always has been. The balance of trust vs respect - he needs to trust that I'm a good, safe leader but I also needs the respect of an animal 10 times my size! It's about pressure and release, be a dick = pressure on... less of a dick = pressure off! I love how super his attitude is to work though and I will be keeping these initial sessions to 20 minutes of fun and praise as long as possible!

With my patience tested for the millionth time and Pat being such a golden boy, I wondered often if I had done the right thing doubling my herd. I think you only really know for sure when you get on them, when you feel that initial reaction to what you're asking, that connection of being on their back. Are they going to listen and respond or are they going to destroy your last hope of ever falling in love…? Well it wasn't until week five that I braved wriggling on, it's funny because I have this uncanny ability to detach myself from horses that aren't mine and I don't feel scared. Apprehensive, maybe, but not terrified like I have been getting on Pat some days. Bender although he belongs to me, doesn't quite feel 'mine' yet. He is a gentle soul but I have a feeling there is a little stubbornness in there too.

♥ Friday, October 6, 2017

Educating Bender week 5! What a happy Friday, after wriggling on him for a sit after a ride and lead the other day I knew it was only a matter of time before I was properly astride my love. He had Weds/Thurs off whilst I was at HOYS so today I tacked him up, lunged for 10 minutes over his usual 3 poles on a curve arrangement in the field. He was keener today, usually he is a slug and takes a lot of vocal encouragement on the lunge but having brought the mounting block down, it was now or never. He stood stock still whilst I wriggled on, I sat up and worked out the best way to make him move without me needing a parachute!

Ordinarily you would have someone on the ground leading at this stage but I don't have that luxury in the daylight- I am usually alone. I clicked, nothing! I tried turning, nothing! I wiggled and joyfully repeated "walk on", nothing! I had to use my leg, lord knows this horse is likely to only have been ridden with a racing saddle on and won't have felt 11st of porky wimp nudging his ribs, but he responded as though he had been in a riding school for years! Obedient and calm. We did 4/5 circles on each rein, tons of praise for him softening into the bend and I then asked for trot... He trotted, it was a wonderful feeling. Unbalanced but he's so solid it's not unnerving.

3/4 circles of trot on each rein and over the poles!! Massive cuddles and lots of treats for Bendy Wendy today!!! I'm so, so happy with him. I also took Pat out for a hack to test our fitness ready for autumn hunting TOMORROW!!! And having given Bender some fibre nuggets in the field, he barely whinnied! Such a huge improvement on his field pacing and screaming!! So Pat is going hunting tomorrow and another little ride for Bendy.

There it was, the start of ridden work for my 'unridden' ex-racehorse. He is such a gent and not at all the sharp prickle that Pat can be. But you heard it correctly, I was hunting tomorrow… HUNTING. The last time I did that was with the Kent and Surrey Bloodhounds last Christmas and I jumped a 5ft hedge!! This time it was set to be much more sedate so I wasn't sweating too profusely.

HUNTING REPORT

So here it is... day one of my autumn/winter regime, Autumn hunting with the Burton Hunt. With the meet being at 3.30pm and only 500yrds from home, I had all morning to fret. I woke up early and went back to bed with a book, a cat and a bucket of tea! At 12pm I was prematurely dressed and ready to go so I delivered pink parcels to the post office and stopped in for a cheeky swifty at the pub next door. I rather annoyingly bought and smoked a ciggie, but by Jove it calmed my jiggly belly!

I got up to the yard and went to ride my Bender before getting Pat ready for the off. Totally took my mind off hunting and I really enjoyed our first little canter. All the ponies brought in, I brushed Pat and tacked him up. Our chaperone for the day was our trusty Grain Pirate Dan (husband to Aunty Smurph) and he too was ready to rock and/or roll!!!!

We mounted and rode the 10 minutes to the meet in which time I had guzzled half my flask and smoked another cigarette!! I turned around and Grain Pirate was swigging whisky from an Evian bottle... I haven't laughed so much in ages!! This is how we roll!!! I had one glass of red at the meet and we were ready for the off!! Pat was terribly excited and wouldn't trot anywhere, canter was all he could muster even on the road, silly bum!!

We had a good blast and jumped a few jumps that all were nice and familiar so didn't scare us too much, then standing at the covert Pat was not for stationary momentum. He was READY FOR ACTION!! At this point my bum twitched slightly, he was silly and I was a bit scared and it was like telepathy... Daddy Carrot came round the corner (foot following) with an apple and all was well again.

We jumped a couple more fences and a small hedge and flew down the side of a field of maize with very little control but guess what...? I wasn't frightened, not a jot!! I had the frigging time of my life!!! We stayed out until dusk, finished my flask and met some really lovely people. What a wonderful warm welcome we had, thank you so, so much to The Burton Hunt and to their Supporters Club who made the most delicious burgers and sausages for supper afterwards. I cannot wait to be out again.

Love as always

Vic and Pat xxxxx

Sobbing tears of joy this morning writing this book, my very first BE event was a year ago this weekend and I cried tears of fear for a week before that day, we've come so far and I'm so proud of what I've achieved in my brain area. You really can do anything to set your mind to and I know it!!! You really can, not only could I not face getting on my horse; I was often shy, introvert and even avoided food shopping at busy times. I didn't like making a fuss or feeling like an inconvenience and I expect being able to achieve so much in one area of my life has led to the confidence growth in another. I am now one of the most out spoken people I know, I will make conversation with anyone and I can finally be myself without feeling guilty for it. I know my own mind now and what makes me happy and what doesn't. I'm not afraid to have a different opinion to someone else either.

My life has changed a lot in the last year, I now work from home, I have my own business (something I should have done years ago but never had the balls) and I am very content. There are still days where I feel very alone in my thoughts but that is 100% normal and I have learnt to be content with that.

On a business front, I know there will be many people reading this that wish their career was more exciting, you wish you had done something different or didn't have to do a job you're not passionate about. Well I'll tell you what.... WHAT THE F*CK ARE YOU WAITING FOR?! 40+ hours a week is a long time to spend wishing you were somewhere else.

And don't think for a second I had a net to catch me if it all went up the badger's backside... I had no windfall, rich parents or savings account. Nothing changed for me financially in order for me to do this, the only thing that changed was having the confidence to do it. I had about £600 in the bank as a buffer for the next month's bills, I saved this up over 2 months by selling anything not nailed down and knowing that I only had a month to build the business up I got to work straight away! I haven't ever wished I could go back, not once. It was the absolute, best decision I have ever made. I worked 10 years for other people, 10 years of being instructed by directors that didn't ever understand 'my' vision, just theirs.

The only thing I do regret is not doing it much sooner. I was probably good enough to go freelance in marketing 5 years ago, but I didn't believe in myself. I had controlling bosses that were very demanding and I always felt downtrodden even though sometimes I was more skilled than them. Now that I have that confidence, I use It wisely and as long as you are prepared to work harder than you have ever worked and for just enough to get by… you might just be a lot happier? Give me beans on toast eaten with a smile any day of the week… Leave unhappy steak eating for politicians!

The basics; Life is too short to spend it worrying about a job you hate. You don't get another go at life, why not make something monumental of it?

Look at the bigger picture, what have you actually got to lose? Your dignity? Well mine b*ggered off when I told the public about my frequent toilet habits… Dignity is over-rated, happiness is what really matters.

Make it happen don't wait for it to fall in your lap, YOU CAN DO THIS, I BELIEVE YOU CAN because I did and I know what it takes. Don't give up. You owe it to yourself.

♥ Friday, September 29, 2017

It's FRIDAAAAY!!!!! I've just woken up in my third hotel room in 4 days but today it is for VERY EXCITING reasons!! I enjoyed a lovely late dinner and drinks with an old friend last night and we reminisced about pony times gone by. It was wonderful, I love taking myself back 5 years and looking at how much different things are now. I woke up this morning so determined to make the next 5 years just as monumental. Starting RIGHT now. It is so important to grab life by the big hairy *b*llocks as soon as you can. It's refreshing, gives you a buzz like no other and can truly make you feel alive. I'm grabbing today, and tomorrow and the day after... I feel different, I feel totally in control of my own fate and you can too.*

I have just spent a few minutes (WAY longer!!!) browsing photos, I have chosen 3. The first is where I've come from. The innocence, the filthy face, the loving family and grounded hard working roots that have always been in me somewhere and always will be. The second; a photo of me doing something I never thought possible JUMPING A BLOODY GREAT JUMP*- the present. I am* NOT *brave, I couldn't do it every day but I know I* CAN *do it. And finally the future, happiness- the end goal, what it all boils down to, smiling at my husband in front of our little house.*

Look at where you've come from, what motivates you and what you want from life. WHAT DO YOU ACTUALLY WANT*???? Be honest with yourself. Feel the buzz, the passion, the love and work for it. I believe in doing as much as you can for as little in return (I'm no Lord Sugar!!) because on this basis you will be wealthy in far more areas than money. You will be repaid in gratitude, loyalty and love, and isn't that what really makes us rich?*

*Go, make a start today, feel inspired, be fearless and remember don't give two sh*ts what people think if they're p*ssing on your chips... they'll wish they were nicer when you fly off on a magic carpet of success without the smell of urine! Fly free my loves,* YOU *(and only you) are in control of today.*

THE END IS NIGH

With only one event left, I started feeling a little bit sad and despondent that I hadn't managed to bring myself to enter another BE100 before the end, it's likely that we were capable I just didn't feel ready mentally to put that kind of pressure on myself and I would have hated to have a bad run so late on with no way of fixing it. Our confidence is so fragile that if I broke it, it might be that I never signed up for eventing EVER again! And who's keeping tabs anyway, I like 90, I feel safe there and that is where I plan to remain for next season too. Maybe even an 80 to get us going. It's about me and my horse, b*gger what other people think.

I had heard my last event at Norton Disney was set to be one of the kindest on the circuit so I looked forward with excitement this time not full of dread to the week's countdown.

We went to our regular outing in the week leading up to the D Day BE Day, this time it was evening dressage where we celebrated a super win in the Elementary class and a second place in the Novice. What a confidence boost. I even got on from the side of the trailer without any help too!!! SHOCK HORROR – I wouldn't have done that 8 months ago! That brim full confidence was short lived though, why does it have to be so bloody hard?

♥ Wednesday, October 18, 2017

So here's the thing... I went to dressage Friday and what with one thing and another (avoidance), I didn't ride Saturday, Sunday, Monday or Tuesday - not once, not either of the horses!!! Yep that's right! I have my last BE event this Sunday and I can't even get on and go for a mooch round the block FFS!!!! One step forward blah blah blah!!!

I woke up this morning and felt lethargic, I felt stale, I felt like I just want to keep pet ponies not riding ones!! But something hit me, it was around 10am... something spurred my soulless arse into gear. I got dressed in actual jodhpurs and seized the moment! It was like something inside me took over. I arrived at the yard expecting a royal fuss when taking Pat away from Bender but NOTHING!!! A whinny and then head down eating. I think I may have been looking for excuses...

I tacked him up, I got ready and off we went, off the yard in the wrong direction! (I usually go the same way because superstition tells me I will survive going right and not left!) but in for a penny! I trotted for 15 minutes, cantered for 5 and then had a walk break, back into trot I dared myself to jump a set of rails outside Auntie Smurph's house and we did it!!! Another stretch of canter and another set of rails and wall (which by the way, was my goal jump when I first arrived here!!) WE JUMPED IT... perfect stride, galloped away down the field together, so merrily skipping along I could have cried!

Back into canter up another field and lined him up at a hedge... he backed off it a bit and I almost wished I hadn't done it but I was there 'Yip Yipping' and we bloody flew that one too!!! We walked home grinning from ear to ear after the best ride I've had in forever.

Now I know it's not hugely safe to jump alone like that but there were farm workers around and I had my phone, Daddy Carrot got my compulsory "I'm hacking" photo and would be awaiting my safe return text!! But what a frigging ride! After all week of building it up, of dodging the most wonderful bullet... I bit it and it was GREAT!!!

If like me, you are dreading it today, grab this nugget of courage and run like the wind for your saddle...you can do it. I know you can! I hope you have a just as wonderful ride and fill your heart back up with happiness, I'm full to the brim and very happy to share it xxx

I do this a lot, avoid riding because the thought of it can fill me with dread even now. But I get there and get on and even if it isn't a good ride, I have never ever regretted a single second in the saddle, ever. That's the point isn't it – the pressure we put on ourselves, if we couldn't ever ride again… how much would you wish you had just one more go at it.

I've been writing this book that you are reading for weeks now and I have told myself that this crucial week to get it completed, that I am not allowed to ride until it's finished. Well, I've cleaned my tack ready, picked out my new boots for Pat and Bender and I'm just slogging through the last few chapters because I WANT TO RIDE. I actually want to. – You're probably best not to read any further because I'll be rushing it and it'll likely be full of typos!

So here it is, the very last one, the grand finale, the home straight.

BUT WAIT…

♥ Saturday, October 21 2017

What is our weak point...? Skinnies... Just walked the course and guess WHAT!!!! 5 out of 18 jumps for tomorrow's Dday BEday are slippery little skinnies. I'm loose in the leavings but CHALLENGE ACCEPTED!!!

EVENT REPORT – Norton Disney BE90

So here goes... (tissues advisory, wine compulsory) I'm struggling to know where to start so as usual, I'll take you back to Friday night....

This week had been a write-off, I lacked enthusiasm at the start and finally pulled my finger out of my arse on Thursday with an excellent ride, jump and grin! Friday night I took Grain Pirate Dan for a confidence boosting ride of his life and we sailed the hedge again and a set of rails and had a few good canters. Auntie Smurph and Pirate Dan are our husband and wife neighbours and yard sharers and I'm glad neither of them mind me f'ing and blinding at them when they ride with me...

after all, instilling confidence in people is my main aim in life these days!!

With two good confidence boosting hacks and I was feeling much better about Sunday morning eventing!

Saturday, I got up and went early to walk the course, rather unusually minus a hangover! I came back white as a sheet. 5 skinnies in a course of 18!!! Now, I don't know about anyone else but fear triggers Adrenalin in me and that chemical either spurs me up or knocks me out. Well, I slept for 2 hours when I got home!! By which time Storm Brian Big Blows had come to town, just in time for me to run through my dressage test!!! F*cking salt in the wound my friend, salt in the wound!!!

I trundled down the field and bizarrely Pat couldn't give two sh*ts about Brian and he went the best he's gone in ages!!! I do love him dearly! Everything packed up, pony plaited and all ready for our 6am departure, I went home for fish and chips and a glass of wine!!

At this point I felt okay about not being able to get round the XC, we've got plenty of time to practice over winter and as long as I enjoy the dressage and don't cry getting on it'll have been a good day!

I woke up this morning and my mate Windy Brian was still pounding twigs at my front door, I was so close to bailing out. Auntie Smurph was taxi today and she said it was my call... Urgh! Mine, my decision. After much deliberation on the loo, and a message to my beloved best friend at 5am, I decided to pull my bloody knickers up (literally) and get a grip!!

It was still pretty dark on arrival and after a twitchy bum loose horse moment in the car park where a chestnut figure was careering past us, the mount of death almost brought on a little cry. I was leading him round fretting about it for ages, I'm very lucky with Auntie Smurph; she does not judge me for being scared or irrational or asking strangers for cigarettes!

Finally, I got on and he settled really quickly in the warm up thank you to the Blue Chip Feed calmers!! Into the test and he was so obedient, I had a really lovely ride. We happily plopped round for what I thought deserved a 28ish. Lucky for us we got a 29.3, with a slightly samey sheet of 7s, nothing more, nothing less. He's never got less than an 8 for his free walk but today lucky 8 was what gave us that sub 30 yet again. We were in the top ten marks in the section though so I'm very happy with that.

Now to the phase that permanently lets us down. I was so terribly nervous again, I ran to the green box and stayed for a minute hoping it would lock fast and I'd just have to stay there for the day! I had a cigarette, yep that's right, and I got on... We warmed up and I have to say, I felt 100% more confident than I ever have in this phase. I'm putting that down to the French Knights in Turquoise Capes who came to visit a couple of weeks ago... they brought with them my new Voltaire Design saddle that was now holding my leg in place, keeping me in balance and to be honest I worried so much less...

I went in the ring, I didn't panic, I didn't rush, the fences came one by one and I addressed them all as they happened. And it really was that basic because look…WE WENT F*CKING CLEAR!!!! Clear!!! We went clear! Our second ever affiliated clear round EVER!!! I was so frigging delighted, I can't even put it into words right now.

Oh Crikey! Now it meant something, the course I had resigned myself to getting eliminated at, now meant a placing. URGH!!

The pit of my empty stomach still managed to churn as I got changed for the death phase. On board and into the warm up, I jumped a jump and went to put my number down on the board of people ready to face their doom. However, if I had been wearing my number, I might have been able to!! A quick spin back to the trailer to put my forgotten bib on and I was back warming up trying to pretend not to be flustered. It wasn't that long until I was called over to face my doom.

In the start box I have learnt not to cry or whinge or turn for home and instead just be still, enjoy these last few moments of aliveness and breathe without burping bile.

"5...4...3...2...1"!!! Bang, like a rocket we soared out the box like our pants were on fire!!! Number 1 always jumps cr*p, I never get a good shot and this was no different, it was a green palisade type jump that looked nothing, but by Jove did it make me buck my ideas up! Number 2, a wooden box fence jumped very well indeed, a gallop around the corner to a dip and up a bank to 3, a roll top; I got a lovely jump over that and 'yeehaaared' my way to the croquet set at 4, he backed off that and I howled at him and smacked his shoulder with my whip, he sailed it enormously in reply! The first skinny was 5, off a turn where I knew there was an alternative route, I didn't take it!! I held my line and kicked like b*ggery and over we got!!! YES bloody yes!!!! One down!!! A gallop up to a log for 6 and a skinny log on the mound for 7a, down the bank to 7b, a skinny brush, well who ever said; look straight ahead and mind your knees... I frigging well looked ahead, locked him on and kicked... we flew it!!!! It felt amazing!!!!! I could have stopped there and been ecstatic!

But alas... Down to 8 and 9 a set of double rails and palisade that both flew by without trouble, up to 10, the steps (2 of) ping ping!!! Up we climbed!! Down to 11 another downhill into a box house skinny! We were on bloody fire!!! He soared over it and we were away, I'm pretty sure his neck was sore from all the patting by now! 12 was the coffin and trellis and he popped through no bother on to 13, one I toyed with the alternative again... bugger it, he was jumping for his life today and so was I, we went for the direct route and it paid off!!!! Only one skinny left!!! Yip yip!! There it was, the water barrels! He flew and splashed his way through the water and down to the house at 15! We were going for it now... 16a&b and 17 were all in a line and jumped very nicely with a howl and huge pat we galloped to the last, sailed the shot gun cartridge and burst through the finish!!!!!

Yyeeeeeeeeeeeaaaaaaaaaaaasssssss!! The absolute best ride of my life. I cannot explain that feeling, once you've felt it there's nothing that compares to sailing through the finish line having ridden your heart out to end on your dressage score!!

A double clear!!! I've only ever had one other and that was at Chilham back at the start... it all came together again today!!! What a feeling, what a day, what a horse!! 29.3 double clear!! We finish 6th in our section!!!

I am so immensely grateful for the support and confidence I have been given by every single one of you on this page. This was for you today. You made me this brave, you got me through this BE season and you earned this feeling too. I thank you with everything I have.

Another huge thank you to my wonderful sponsors and everyone else who has supported us this year, I really wouldn't have been able to do it without you. It's humbling that you have taken a gamble with an average rider and her average horse who thanks to you, appear to have become anything but average.

Once again, thank you.

I am sobbing with pride over what we have achieved, anything is possible. Never ever give up on a dream. Ever.

Love, as always

Vic and Pat Xxxx

So that's it my friends, not a dry eye in the house. I get quite emotional these days, every time I think back to the days of hiding my saddle and pretending I forgot it so I didn't have to ride, when every reply to 'did you have a good ride?' was a lie because I didn't even get out of the car. I cry not with sadness but with pride, pride for what I have overcome, or how I still feel a lot of the time and regardless of that fear, I bloody well get on with it. I have never done anything this well or worked this hard in my whole life. That's the point isn't it? Hard work really does pay off. Be passionate, set goals, change goals, make a life to be proud of – what are you waiting for?

♥ Wednesday, October 25, 2017

I have a question for you... I was sat pondering my 2017 eventing season and how far I have come in my confidence. Not just confidence as a rider but as a person. I'm more independent, I'm stronger and more able to love and give help to people because of this strength.

I'd like to know, what is bravery to you? What defines success and failure? For me, bravery is feeling scared out of your skin and still going through the motions, it's giving it all you can despite your crippling fear and learning to enjoy it.

I've learnt to enjoy always being a little bit out of control. We ride horses, you will NEVER be 100% in control. Fact. Learn to have fun, train yourself to smile through a spook or sigh at a stop, the other options are cross stitch or chess... Success is in the tiniest step, less palm sweating, an open field canter, 3 days riding in a row.. it's looking back and realising how little you thought you could achieve at the beginning.

18 months ago I thought I'd never ever enjoy getting on my horse ever again, I never imagined smiling over a jump or screaming with joy through the XC finish line! I know that I've taken hundreds of tiny steps this year and some massive ones right back to where we started but the success is in the trying.

My biggest success to date is getting on Pat by myself at Shelford BE... my proudest moment to date (normally I get Daddy Carrot to feed and hold so I don't feel so scared). Something so trivial to so many people but such a huge step for me.

*Try to let go, give less of a sh*t what it looks like, what people think, drop the stigma, don't be afraid to look like a d*ckhead... it WILL change your life, I know it will.*

Failure is not an option, as far as I'm concerned it doesn't exist. The only time I will ever fail is if I don't try in the first place... failing off isn't failure, nor is coming last, learn from it and you will never fail again.

The opportunities that have opened up to us because of this public display of fear conquering have been amazing. I was very kindly offered and accepted a column in a national equestrian magazine and by the time you read this you will likely know which one (the best one!!). I have been invited to some amazing places to do some brilliant things; taking the course walk at Blenheim Palace Horse Trials for Falpro was a highlight with memories I will treasure forever. We have lots to look forward to as well. I have signed some wonderful contracts for next year with some impressive companies that will help me to grow this mission I am on. I won't stop until I know I can't help people anymore. As long as what I write gets people out of bed, keeps them smiling and helps them worry less – what more can I ask for?

So, what does the future hold for us?

Well Pat will have a rest, he likes to be doing a job so it won't be too long but I will let his fitness down for November and December ready to start getting him back to work in January for next season (Yep! That's right, there's a 'next season'!). I have loved the eventing community for the most part and next year we will be campaigning hard to make sure the equestrian community is kind and welcoming for everyone that wants to have a go, whether it's eventing, showing or just hacking to the pub. Our Wimpy world is growing and it provides a safe place full of encouraging people to help each other and that's what it's all about.

Bender will be developing his gentlemanly nature and hopefully his confidence in being alone so that we can enter into the world of SHOWING. This is new for me, I haven't done a lot of showing but I have the rather ambitious goal of riding at The Horse of the Year Show so I better work as hard at this as I have at eventing this year! And if he doesn't want to do that, we'll just go hacking instead!

Daddy Carrot is going to ride a little more if he can find some suitable underpants. I think he is much happier being chief in charge of studs and photography though!

And I will be practicing my show jumping, writing more, learning to make decent Yorkshire puddings and making every day the best that it can be. From now on, I will be living life for us, for my boys and not in fear of other people's judging eyes.

Look back often at your life and how far you have come but don't linger. If there is something in life that you want to achieve you must first make a plan (do it TODAY), you need to work hard for it like you've never worked before and adapt your plans along the way. You must also remember to tread your own path because although a trodden path may be easier to walk down, there is likely nothing left for you at the end.

You cannot change what has already been, but you can make what hasn't happed yet downright bloody brilliant. You have that power, the power to change YOUR tomorrow – what is it that you're waiting for?

Over the page there is a list of things for you to remember, things to remind yourself of. These things will keep you going when you face a rocky road or difficult chapter, for when you need it most. Read them – out loud if you can, keep in mind those things and take those bold steps forward, you won't ever regret anything you can learn from.

Important things to remember Part II

You know the drill, tear it out and keep it on your person…

Something that is absolutely pivotal in aiding confidence for those riding, competing, tobogganing, etc. is knowing that it is ABSOLUTELY 100% FINE TO F*CK IT UP... if you don't die, you can only learn from it.

The bottom line is, those that mind don't matter and those that matter don't mind. The people that I love and who love me; they are supportive, they are encouraging, and they are worth one hundred of every single one of the Chip P*ssers!

I have been scared, I have felt fear, I have been consumed by worry and stress to the point where I cannot think ahead of that day or even hour without feeling overwhelmed. It's more common than you think and it is NOTHING to be ashamed of.

Fake smiles are easy to detect when you start smiling real ones that burst with joy, remember that.

It's much better for your own mental health to live a life never judging or keeping score. Putting other people's feelings first will make you feel fulfilled in a way no chocolate bar or glass of wine ever can.

My advice to anyone thinking of getting an ex-racehorse (or any horse for that matter) is that if you don't have the patience to complete a rubix cube wearing a blindfold, forget it!

It might appear sometimes, that other people have far great chances of success than you because of what they have. Material possessions and a wonderful indoor school won't get you anywhere without hard work.

Look at the bigger picture, what have you actually got to lose? Your dignity? Well mine b*ggered off when I told the public about my frequent toilet habits… Dignity is over-rated, happiness is what really matters.

Make it happen don't wait for it to fall in your lap, YOU CAN DO THIS, I BELIEVE YOU CAN because I did and I know what it takes. Don't give up. You owe it to yourself.

Don't ever think for a second that you get anywhere in life without sacrifice and hard work.

Be passionate, set goals, change goals, make a life to be proud of – what if there wasn't going to be a tomorrow, then what would your today look like?

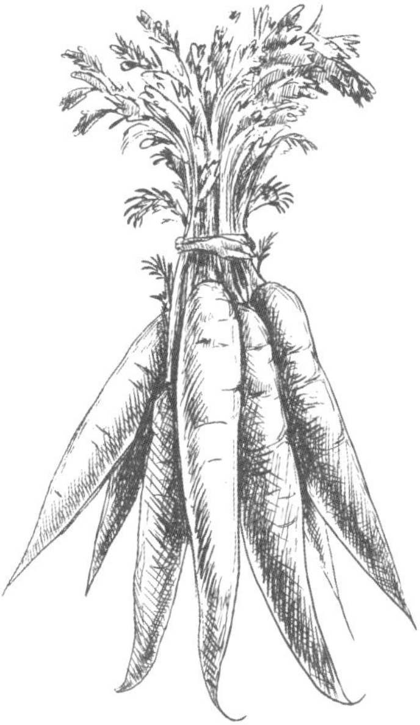

A CARROT'S EYE VIEW:

AN INTERVIEW WITH DADDY CARROT

Sum up eventing in ten words or less

It isn't as bad as watching dressage on its own.

Describe a day out eventing with your wife and her horse.

It starts way before the actual day with a gradual build-up of apprehension. The night before usually means her drinking more than I would if I had to get up at 5am, travel three hours and then ride all day. First thing in the morning my wife tends to sneak out of bed and disappear into the toilet for a while. Sometimes more than once.

Even though we get up at the crack of sparrow's fart, there is never any time to eat anything or have a cup of tea. We go straight down to the yard where hopefully she's loaded all of her cr*p in the horsebox the night before so we don't have to linger about too long. She won't let me drive her precious cargo so we have to drive at around 10mph and it takes far too long to get there.

On arrival she will always scurry off to some tent next to the bacon roll tent, but there's no time for bacon – I know not to ask this anymore. Next, we go back to the lorry and she dresses him up in diamonds. She is NOT chatty at this point. I am usually left in the rain holding the horse while she visits the toilet again.

The first part of the day is down in a grass field about a mile and a half from the horse box. There are loads of people trotting and walking and trotting and walking and trotting and walking. It's like watching paint dry. At this point I take photos of her warming up, which apart from the other riders in the background, look exactly like the photos of the test.

When she gets near the white planks they beep a car horn, which is good because then I know the actual test has started.

I know it's finished when she's smiling and heading towards me.

We go back to the horsebox (back past the food vendors from earlier – I mentally note what's on offer and bide my time) then she changes clothes and the boring bit is officially over. Hopefully we haven't parked too far away from each bit, because walking ten miles isn't much fun when you haven't got a horse to help you.

In the show jumping warm up (which is always near the food vendors) my job is to stand at the most dangerous spot in the middle and put the poles back on the jumps after she knocks them down. Invariably this means I become the official show jumping warm-up helper, picking up the poles for EVERYONE. Tedious. Around this stage she will appear slightly less nervous, but may still snap at me if I get in the way.

Show jumping is probably the easiest bit to spectate. I have no idea what's happening in the dressage and I only see the first and last jump of the cross country. Pole down = bad. Pole still up = good. This appeals to my logic.

Experience has taught me that immediately after the show jumping is the opportune moment to sneak off to get myself some food. She is likely to be far too nervous about the cross country to care where I've gone.

Back at the horse box for the final wardrobe change of the day. This time into something far more protective than a piece of tweed cloth. By now she has usually lost a bit of the nervous tension and has subsided into a kind of morbid acceptance of certain death.

I watch her over the first couple of jumps on the course which seem to be a bit smaller and easier than the middle ones and then wait for her to come back to the finish. I like to find out the optimum time for the course and keep track on my watch. She usually goes too fast but it doesn't matter because at the finish she becomes what I like to call, "High on Horse". She's finally enjoying herself now it's over!

Back at the horsebox I am almost ready for another bacon roll, but we have to wash him, put him in pyjamas, wrap stuff on his legs. Sometimes I get given a "manly" job like taking out the studs, thus warranting my presence for the last six hours.

Then we check the scores and see where she has finished, which can sometimes be a long wait for absolutely nothing. However, without fail she will always purchase several photographs to take home, despite me having well over 100 (free) pictures on the camera I brought with me.

What have you learnt most?

It is usually best not to say too much until the cross country is over. Just remain silent and close to hand like a dust pan and brush.

I have learnt not to arrange anything else on an event day. Despite what time she says you'll be done and home, it takes ALL day.

I've learnt that flip flops are frowned upon as event day attire. Turning up on a motorbike is also frowned upon.

The catering vans usually do the rounds of all the local events. Establish your favourite and stick with it. With a bit of luck, the vendor may come to recognise your loyalty and reward you with extra bacon.

Most of all, I admire my wife for her passion and dedication and what she has achieved. I actually quite enjoy going and watching her ride and it isn't anywhere near as unbearable as I have just made out.

P.S. Always have a carrot in your pocket.

Love as always

Vic and Pat xxx

(And Bender and Daddy Carrot)